Teenagers Talk About

SUICIDE

To Bobbie

Teenagers Talk About SUICIDE

MARION CROOK

NC Press Limited
Toronto, 1988

Canadian Cataloguing in Publication Data

Crook, Marion, 1941-
  Teenagers talk about suicide

Bibliography: p
ISBN 1-55021-013-0

1. Suicide.   2. Youth – Suicidal behavior.
I. Title.

HV6546.C76 1988   616.85'8445071   C88-093289-9

The author wishes to acknowledge the Canadian Mental Health Association (B.C. division) and the Vancouver Crisis Centre for their assistance in the research, development and completion of this book.

We would like to thank the Ontario Arts Council and the Canada Council for their assistance in the production of this book.

New Canada Publications, a division of NC Press Limited, Box 4010, Station A, Toronto, Ontario, Canada, M5W 1H8.

Distributed in the United States of America by Independent Publishers' Group, 814 North Franklin Street, Chicago, Illinois, 60610.

Printed and bound in Canada

Cover Design: Don Fernley

CONTENTS

ACKNOWLEDGEMENTS

I would like the thank all the teens who responded to my ads in the newspapers and called or met with me. Without the grants from the **Chris Spencer Foundation** and **The Van Dusen Society** I would not have been able to travel to see you. The **Canadian Mental Health Association (B.C. Division)** and the **Suicide Information and Education Centre** in Calgary, the **Distress Centre** in Toronto and the **Helpline** in Halifax gave me practical help and encouragement. **Carol Lowe,** Program Director of the **Vancouver Crisis Centre,** gave me much needed advice and information over the many months it took to prepare the manuscript. I would like to thank **Peter Gajdis, Julie Epp** and **Angela Haggerty** who reviewed my questions and the chapter on suicide risk and offered invaluable advice. **Jasha Ramsay,** Executive Director of the Vancouver Crisis Centre gave me initial encouragement and continual support. Thanks to **Chloe Lapp, Canadian Mental Health Association, Gordon Winch** and **Ila Rutlege, Toronto Distress Centre,** as well as **Mathew and Ashley Lindsay** of Winnipeg who boarded me and introduced me to their friends.

FOREWORD

I did not want to write this book. I was happily writing fiction, researching stories in airplanes, tugboats, gold fields, ranches, and interesting corners of life around me. I knew teenagers tried suicide. I knew you were having a difficult time living but I didn't see that it was *my* problem. I had teenagers at home who needed time and attention. I didn't need any more of you. That's what I thought.

Then I wrote a book about how teenagers feel about being adopted *THE FACE IN THE MIRROR: Teenagers Talk About Adoption*, NC Press Limited, 1986 and, when I researched that, I talked to forty teens. They were interesting and I got some idea of what life was like for you.

One night, about two months after that book was on the shelves, I got a telephone call from a woman who had read my adoption book and wanted me to take her daughter's diary and make a book from it. Her daughter had kept a diary and a journal, snippets of ideas and some poems, from the time she was sixteen until twenty-one when she killed herself. The girl's brother had also killed himself earlier. Their mother thought that, if I could study Bobbie's written work, I might find out why she had killed herself and be able to help others. I said, "No, I can't do it. I'm not a psychiatrist. I don't know enough." Bobbie's mother sent her daughter's writing anyway. I didn't read it. I kept it on the floor of my study for months. I moved from the interior of British Columbia to the coast, packing the writings with me. I still didn't do anything about them, except let my conscience work on the information until I finally felt I had to do *something*.

I couldn't write about Bobbie. I didn't feel I could know her well enough or that even telling only her story would help readers much. But I thought that teenagers who had tried suicide and not completed it could tell me what made suicide seem like such a good idea. So, with the publisher behind me, I approached the Vancouver Crisis Centre. I hoped they'd tell me not to write it. Wouldn't such a book encourage teens to try suicide? No. They told me that no one wants to talk about suicide. Everyone wants to pretend that it doesn't happen, or it happens by accident. Teens need more information. They need to know what to look for, what to beware of, where to go.

Next I went to the Canadian Mental Health Association. The Executive Director there told me she really wanted me to do the research and write the book and that she and her office staff would do all they could to help me. It seemed as though there was a tremendous need for this book. That you, teenagers, needed a book that was yours, one that reported to you what other teens felt, what they wanted, how they coped. I felt as though I'd tentatively put my foot in the water and a strong current was pulling me under.

So, with the assistance of the Chris Spencer Foundation, the Van Dusen Foundation, the Canadian Mental Health Association (B.C. Division), a group of three young people in Vancouver, (my advisory board), and the Distress Centre in Toronto, I started interviewing.

I was afraid that the plan I had, the questionnaire, would not be good enough, that I would have to phone everyone I interviewed and, months later, ask vital questions I hadn't thought of until I had finished the research. I received advice from a medical researcher who listened to my plans and told me to go ahead, I was on the right track. At this point I needed a lot of encouragement.

I couldn't put off the project any longer. I had to get out there and ask you what I needed to know.

I spent the summer of 1987 in fast food restaurants across Canada interviewing teenagers. I advertised in the paper and you called in, willing to talk to me, willing to tell me what other teens should know. I met you at McDonald's on Yonge Street in Toronto, at McDonald's in downtown Winnipeg, at the Burger King, Swenson's, on park benches, in your homes. I sat in the sun on Granville Island in Vancouver and talked to one of you for two hours. I got lost in Calgary driving around the cemetery three times trying to find a house. I sat on a bench in Trinity Square in Toronto growing colder by the minute as the sun set behind tall buildings and you told me what it was like to be so alone that death was better than any life you could imagine. I couldn't meet all who called me. Sometimes I was only in that city for three days and I could only see three of you each day. I had to go off by myself for at least an hour between interviews. I couldn't listen to that much emotion without absorbing some of it and I needed a little time to bring my own emotions into equilibrium. It was a long summer.

But you inspired me. I admired your courage. I admired your independence. I admired your ability to finally believe in yourselves. So many of you were truly fine people, courageous, generous. But in a way, that only made my problems worse. You joined the personnel of the Crisis Centre and the Mental Health Association and the Foundations adding your voices to theirs, your expectations to theirs. Everyone wanted me to write what would be useful and important. You made me work very hard.

I found you in your homes living with your parents. Sometimes they didn't know that you had tried suicide and you didn't want me to tell them. I respected that. Sometimes your parents respected your privacy and we talked in your house while your parents stayed in the backyard, or in the kitchen and never came in to ask me why I was there. I was amazed that they were so understanding. Sometimes, you knew your parents would never understand and, without telling them, you met me downtown. Sometimes I met you after work on your way home. I met you in The Eaton Centre in Toronto, at the Conservatory in Vancouver, on the only hill I saw in Calgary, on the dock in Halifax.

I thought that food was going to be a big budget item in my research, that you would need food at every interview. I live with two teenage boys of my own and they inhale food. But only occasionally, if we happened to be meeting at lunch, would you have a hamburger with me. The fast-food restaurants got a lot of coffee and pop sales but you were much more interested in talking to me than in eating.

You talked for hours. An interview usually lasted an hour and a half. The shortest was forty minutes and that was because I had to leave to catch a plane. The longest was two hours and forty-five minutes and I felt privileged with each one.

I tried not to read much of the literature before I talked to you. I tried not to read what professional helpers thought about teenagers and suicide. I didn't want my ideas to be shaped by adults. After talking to ten or eleven teens I started to see how life hemmed you in, oppressed you; how you saw few choices. Each one of you told me a different story but often you had similar problems.

This book talks about the teens I met, what your problems were, how you coped with them, what you thought teens should do, what you thought parents and helpers should do. It's not a "study" of teenagers. It's the story of some teenagers. These stories aren't a bible. They don't reveal all the problems there are, or the only ways there are to solve them. These stories are glimpses into other people's lives. Read them and think about them, and feel what it would be like to be that teenager.

Near the end of the book I write about what help is available, what might be useful, how teens might be better able to cope. This book is not a dramatization of the horrors of teen life. It is the reality of that life. Readers should not be discouraged by these stories. They should understand better what they feel when they think of suicide, what their friends feel. And they should be better able to cope with these feelings when they do understand.

I want readers to participate in this book and feel that they are richer, more capable, wiser than they were before they read it. I don't want teens to disappear from life in suicide.

1

WHY TRY SUICIDE?

Round the corner
Hide from the darkness
that follows my footsteps
that lives on my fears
— Megan

When you thought of suicide, most of you felt alone. You felt you were trapped in a small section of life and that you would never get out. Everything seemed hopeless and you felt helpless to find a way out of the mess you were in. Helen said, "It's like you're in a big hole and you're trying to crawl out and the dirt just keeps falling in around you."

Why do so many of you try suicide as a way out? Often, you had more than one reason. Usually, your emotional problems had been growing over the years: rejection, indifference, lack of nurturing, lack of caring. Your life experiences laid problem upon problem like the layers in a refuse dump, until all the problems sifted into one another and smothered you.

Coping with the increasing problems got harder and harder. You managed to deal with the first problem, perhaps the second or third problem, always trying to find a way out. But the seventeenth problem or the twenty-second problem was overwhelming and you only wanted out, wanted to escape living, to escape pain, to escape the pressures of dealing with another day, another problem. Suicide looked like the way out.

Amy was nineteen years old, slim, with dark blonde hair. I interviewed her in the rec-room of her employer. Amy works as a baby-sitter in a private home. She minds the little children, does some of the housework and likes it because the family is warm, and affectionate and accepting. The woman of the house nodded to me when I arrived and disappeared upstairs. She interrupted us only once when she came in to remove one of the children who had wandered in. Obviously Amy's privacy was respected here.

Amy didn't live with this family. She had a long-term relationship with her boyfriend and lived with him. She was just beginning to feel that life held some chance of happiness for her. She told me her troubles started when she was thirteen. They really started before that when she felt her father rejected her and her mother started to reject her, to blame Amy for not being the "perfect daughter." Amy saw it as all happening at thirteen, the summer her mother sent her to stay with relatives.

"I went to the country the summer after grade eight. My mom figured that, oh, she figured all sorts of stuff about me. In grade eight I tried smoking. I tried smoking pot. And that was it. I hated booze. Guys made me nervous. My mom thought I was a drug addict, an alcoholic because she caught me the first time I ever drank anything. She was going to send me to A.A. [Alcoholics Anonymous]. She thought I was so screwed up.

"My mom figured I was a raving nymphomaniac. But I was afraid of guys! I was still a virgin. She thought I was so terrible that she sent me to some strict relatives that would change me. It just screwed me up even more because my mother told my relatives that about me and . . . my cousin figured if I was like that he could have me. My own cousin! That kind of shocked me."

Me: Did he succeed?

"No, but my uncle did. That was really deadly. Relatives try it all the time. Not as bad as that but they like to dance with me at dances and pull me close. Just telling you stuff like this, blows my mind. Pretty strange."

Me: You couldn't get away from your uncle?

"I was at his summer cottage. Not much I could do. Can't walk very far through the bush. The thing was it was my first period time too and I was really nervous. It was scary.

"The thing that really fried me was that I told my mom about it when I got home and she didn't believe me. She phoned my uncle and laughed and said, 'You'll never believe what Amy said this time.'"

Me: How old were you then?

"Thirteen.

"After that, I lived on the streets. Not downtown Vancouver [but a suburb]. I always had big people watching over me. All the welfare bums. I just slept wherever, in apartments, someplace. I got taken care of really good. I was super lucky. I never once had to do anything bad. I never had to hook or anything like that. The worst thing I ever did was sell a few grams of hash for somebody for lunch. And that was it. Never had to do anything. I had so many friends."

From age thirteen to sixteen Amy lived sometimes at home, sometimes in foster homes, sometimes on the street.

Me: And then you tried suicide.

"I felt there was nothing left. There was no school. I wasn't in school. I wasn't going to have a place to live. I didn't have any relatives to count on. My brothers turned their backs on me. They thought I'd run away, but my mother kicked me out.

"I wanted out of life. I didn't think there was anything there for me. I tried suicide once or twice to get back at my parents. Like, you only hurt so much and you just get to a point where you feel absolutely nothing. When I was like that, if my mom or dad would have come up to me and said, 'We're sorry. We want you home.' I would have said, 'No way. Just go away. My parents? I don't care.' I would have meant it. You get to that point and it just doesn't matter.

"I knew that if I killed myself I was just not going to exist. I was just going to go somewhere. At that point I thought I'd rather take a risk, take a chance. Maybe wherever I go will be better. And if not, nothing, just emptiness, would be better than what I had.

"I didn't think there was anything else I could do [except suicide]. I've always thought that family was everything to you, you know. Not any more, but I did then. And, when that was gone, when I knew my parents didn't care, I figured all my friends have families to go to and I don't. They're all in school and I'm not. They're all getting good educations. I've been kicked out. I felt like I'd been kicked out of everything. I didn't think anyone would miss me."

Although some of you had serious problems in your lives early, at ages six or ten, most of you ran into hopelessness around thirteen. You had little or no experience in dealing with problems. Unless your parents took the time to work out problems with you, you couldn't know how. You knew the rest of the world seemed to manage so you watched other kids and tried their solutions. Sometimes the solutions didn't work. You read, and tried a solution you found in a book. Sometimes, not often, but sometimes, you asked a counselor. But usually, you tried to muddle through on your own. And you made mistakes, sometimes, humiliating, painful mistakes. Some parents said, "Oh, you'll grow out of it." You felt they didn't understand because it was not their pain.

Some teens are not devastated by pain. You look around you and you can see that some teens don't understand why *anyone* would consider suicide. People are so different. Some people can wear a jacket on a hot day and the heat never bothers them. Some people come to school in freezing weather without a jacket because the cold doesn't bother them. Everyone is sensitive to heat and cold to some degree, but not to the same degree. Everyone is sensitive to pain, to criticism, to degradation, but some of you are more sensitive than others. Some of you can shrug off your mistakes, learn from them and go on. Some of you feel your failures are crushing, and you brood and worry about how weak, how socially stupid and how empty a person you are. You need a stable, secure emotional life. You need to be surrounded by approval. Anything less and you get out of tune with life and suffer. You often feel a special sensitivity to the emotional life of your families. And you feel responsible for your family.

Sometimes you thought you had to control the family.

Robert was eighteen, intelligent-looking with dark eyes, dark hair and broad shoulders. He must be good-natured because I kept him waiting one hour the first time we tried to meet because I couldn't find the right donut shop. We tried again two weeks later.

I was more successful this time and Robert gave me two and a half hours of his time. He lived at home with his parents and his brother and worked as an actor and film producer in a small, ambitious film company. He felt unappreciated at home but was unable to move out because his father continually borrowed money from him until Robert had no savings. Robert continued to lend it to him. Robert seemed to have some insight into his problems.

He had tried to get help for his family. "My parents suggested that I go to a psychiatrist but that was more to ease their conscience than anything else. I said, 'Look. You guys are fighting all the time now, every hour. Let's all go to a counselor.' So we went once. My dad's not one to change but he went with us. I know my parents play off me. I'm always the bad guy. Mom says, 'Your dad doesn't want you to do this.' And my dad says, 'Your mother doesn't want you to do this.' And then they go, 'Well, who do you believe?' Well, I don't believe either one of them. Then they get upset with me and the whole thing starts all over again. We went a couple of times to the psychiatrist and that was it. My dad said that my mom didn't want to go any more and my mom said my dad didn't want to go anymore. My dad said it was all you guy's fault. All the children's fault. I know that's not true."

Leslie felt as if she had a great deal of control over her family. "If my dad gave me any attention, my mother would get really upset, start throwing things and stuff. I'd leave. Then they'd get into a fight. So I didn't want to leave. So then they'd argue with me. I'd want to get away so badly but I'd think, 'I can't leave. If I leave they'll fight with each other.' I felt so responsible. I felt like I controlled everybody and everything in the family. I felt old. I thought, 'How can everybody be so immature?' I felt like I was the mother and father and they were the kids." Leslie was twelve. "I felt they had something else to worry about if they worried about me. Something besides each other. At the time it would be both of them against me instead of against each other. It hurt, but it worked."

Sometimes sensitive children understand the problems in the family. More commonly you only feel that everything or something is wrong but you don't know what it is. You might think the problems are your fault.

Some of the world's most creative people are extremely sensitive to pain. They are no less valuable, and no less admirable. Their sensitivity is both their weakness and their strength. It's that sensitivity that allows them to communicate in writing, in painting, in poetry. It is also that sensitivity that shakes them, and discourages them and hurts them.

Suzanne said, "I didn't feel like I belonged in my family. I was so different from everyone else."

Tanya said, "Reality demands that you be strong and 'together.' But I'm not like that. Things touch me that don't touch a lot of other people. I interpret things differently than other people. It's not that I dislike life. I mean this. . . is great. I mean look at this. [We were sitting in a park with children and strolling adults around us.] Look at these happy people. If I could be a happy person, like one of them, then I want to be here. But I'm not happy."

Not all of you who tried suicide are extremely sensitive to pain. It wasn't your vulnerability that caused your problems, it was the number and kind of troubles you had. Some had so many difficulties come at you so quickly that few people could cope without help. And some of you have had difficulties come when everything else in your life was going wrong. Usually, you managed your problems, but just this once, usually when another loss came upon you, you couldn't cope.

Too much rejection and criticism, coupled with increasing troubles at school, sent some of you looking for a way out. And for many, it was suicide.

One eighteen-year-old man told me, "It's the pressure around the house."

Me: What's pressure to you?

"The constant put-downs. Constant fighting. You know you've done something wrong. And people drive it into you that you've done it wrong. You know you've done it wrong and they keep driving it into you. They keep telling me I'm not good enough. One person in the family starts on me, then another has to come over and say, 'Well, you did this wrong.' There's never any real communication, you know. If I start to say why I did it they say, 'I don't want to hear about it.'"

Teresa had tried suicide several times. She talked to me in the basement rec-room at the house of her boyfriend's father. She had been living there since she left home three months previously. The Winnipeg sunshine picked up the reds and browns of the room and made it a very warm and comfortable meeting place. Teresa was a blond, energetic, fairly determined young woman who felt she had had to fight very hard for a chance at love and acceptance. She had not found acceptance at her parents' home. She said, "It was just to the point that I didn't want to be around them [her parents] any more. They said everything the wrong way. I couldn't ask my mom to talk to me. I couldn't say, 'Talk to me about sex,' because that was a taboo word. And I couldn't say it to her. She kept after me all the time and I could never talk to her."

Beth had lived with intelligent, wealthy parents. She constantly tried to live up to her parents' high expectations. "At the time [she tried suicide] I just wanted to go to sleep. I didn't want to worry about it. It was the easiest thing to do. I had choices. I could have run away, I could have stayed on and fought with my parents; I could have done what they wanted. But those things would have been hard. It [suicide] was a cop out. It was easier."

I'm not sure if Beth chose suicide because it was "easier" or because she was convinced that she could not cope with any other option.

Jake and I took the last empty seat on the upper floor of Mc-Donald's on Yonge Street, Toronto. Jake wasn't sure why suicide looked like a way out to him. "I don't know. Just being so alone makes me think of it. Like I work so much [he as two jobs] sixty hours a week . . . well, I just come home and I don't get much sleep and I hate my jobs. It's just I feel so alone. And I wonder if it's really worth it. Like there isn't much happiness there."

I talked to thirty of you about why you tried suicide. Generally, you felt isolated from your families and friends. You felt overwhelmed by your problems and you felt unable to cope with or change your lives. Not all of you felt useless or unnecessary to your families. Not all of you felt your families didn't love you. Most felt you couldn't talk to your families—or to anyone.

Why do you try suicide?

For attention? Or did you really want to die?

I don't think the second reason is more valid than the first. They are both important. If you are so desperate you'll choose to risk dying in order to get help you probably have a desire to escape the pain in suicide. Psychiatrists tell me that most people don't want to die; they want their lives to change and they are desperate for that change.

Sometimes when you tried suicide you didn't really plan to die that time. Sometimes you did. That was not always obvious to parents, teachers, hospital staff or those who cared for you.

Anytime someone tries to die, the world should take that person seriously. You told me about your attempts. Joyce said, "I was just trying to get back at my parents." Yet she took forty-eight ASA tablets. That could have killed her.

Gail said, "I really wanted to end it all," and took a bottle of antibiotics because that was handy. Unless she was allergic to that antibiotic she was unlikely to die, but she didn't know that. So it's hard to tell what you wanted to do from what you actually did. Maybe you didn't really know how many pills it takes to die. Other people should treat all attempts at suicide as serious. All need attention. You are all too valuable to be ignored. There is no such thing as an unimportant suicide attempt. Everyone who tries suicide may die, if not this time, then next time. Everyone should treat their own suicide attempts as serious calls for change, their friends' suicide attempts as desperate cries for help.

What triggered you to try suicide? Many things. A visit to the school counselor was too much for Leslie. "I went to see the counselor. She started talking about my bad grades, skipping school. 'Before you say anything . . . you missed this much school.' Lecture. I started to cry. The counselor said, 'Don't try to manipulate me with tears.'" Leslie left that counselor's office without telling her what was wrong.

For Robert, "A whole bunch of events led up to it. One thing after another, a landslide of things that happened. I'd been going out with this girl for a while and she invited me to visit her at her parents' summer place on the island. I said, 'Can I bring a friend along?' So I brought the friend. The day was okay but all through the entire day she kept flirting with my friend and all. And then she asked us to spend the night. We'd missed the last ferry across and as things progressed, things happened between him and her . . . it was hard . . . I was fifteen. But I think what did it mostly was my friend didn't try to stop it. Just kept going with it, and then the excuses came from both of them. 'Well, it just kind of happened.' It was humiliation. I said, 'Well, let's talk about this.' But they just said, 'This is how I feel about him and this is how he feels about me so there.' I was supposed to take it, just like that. And that's what really clinched it. I took a bottle of aspirin on the ferry ride home the next day."

The events that triggered the suicide attempt usually followed months and sometimes years of unhappiness, frustration and perhaps depression. You knew you were living a emotional life. Sometimes you knew why you were unhappy. But sometimes, you didn't recognize your unhappiness until you suddenly realized how desperately you wanted out of life. Very often, a loss triggered your feelings of desperation. You felt you had no real friend, no helping person, no one to talk to. It was all suddenly too much.

2

WHO TRIES SUICIDE?

Suicide is an increasing problem for the fifteen to nineteen-year-old group. In Canada the rate for suicide in males fifteen to nineteen has increased to five times the 1965 rate. For Canadian women fifteen to nineteen it has increased 2.5 times. In the United States the suicide rate for fifteen to twenty-four-year-old males has increased three times since 1967 and 2.5 times for females.

This is in part because more teenagers are trying suicide and, in part, because society is recognizing more deaths as suicides and not "accidents".

While more young teenaged men complete suicide in this age group (in Canada 9.3 per 100,000 total population, women 3.8 per 100,000) more young women *attempt* suicide (822.9 per 100,000), young men 352.5 per 100,000.

The statistics only reflect the teens that reported their attempts, or who were somehow noticed or helped. Many suicide attempts never get reported. Some of you told me I was the only one who knew. You aren't part of those statistics. Your friends are probably not included. There must be many, many teens who never tell anyone.

The statistician reminds me of a folk tale in which the Court Accountant sat on a wall and watched the giant stalk through the town. His job was to count the bodies on the ground after the giant had passed through. While it might be interesting to know how many people died, it doesn't do much to stop the giant. Perhaps understanding why teenagers try suicide will help prevent deaths in the future.

To find out what was happening in the teen world I traveled across Canada meeting teens in Vancouver, Calgary, Winnipeg, Toronto and Halifax. I put an ad in the "personal" or "information wanted" section of a newspaper I thought teens would read. In most papers, the ad said,

> Teenagers and Suicide
> Writer needs interviews with
> 15 - 19 yr olds for teen book.
> Please call XXX-XXXX

You phoned an answering service and left your name and telephone number and I tried to phone everyone and make an appointment to meet. I wondered if I'd find that all teens who tried suicide have the same personality. Well, you don't. But you do share some common ideas.

Rena was a grade nine student, fifteen, living at home with her parents and quietly eager to help other teens who were troubled about suicide. She had red-brown hair, brown eyes, an elf-like face. She was a good student, and had loving parents who had lost track of her problems when they changed neighborhoods. She had been sexually abused when she was eight years old by the brother of a friend of hers. He told her it was her fault, that all men would treat her like that, that she physically invited it because she was pretty. When Rena reached puberty she was confused about her physical appearance and upset by the move. She had to make new friends. Then, at her new school, she was accused of being a lesbian. Rena didn't know why the other girls started this rumor. She only knew that it isolated her and made life very hard. She didn't know where to go for help so she tried suicide. She usually was loved and accepted in her family but, at this time, she was temporarily ignored in her parent's preoccupation with their own problems.

Bruce, now twenty-four, was habitually ignored and not accepted. He told me about his life on the streets of Vancouver. He hit the streets from the age of ten until he was eighteen when he went to jail. He had been in and out of all the detention homes in the area and finally spent three years in jail. Bruce had to survive a family that fought all the time, a father who left home when he was young but constantly pulled at Bruce to get back at his former wife, and a mother who used Bruce to hurt her former husband. He left them both and "did his own thing," on the streets.

Colleen, in Toronto, was driven by car to our meeting at the Burger King by her mother. Colleen was trying to deal with parents who cared but who didn't allow her a chance to make her own decisions. She felt suffocated by the attention. She had made one suicide attempt. Her mother took that attempt seriously and spent hours listening to her and talking with her. Colleen was one of the rare teenagers I talked to who felt her parents, or at least her mother, cared.

Some kids had one parent at home and no brothers or sisters. Some had brothers and sisters and parents but no one who they felt cared about them. Some had alcoholic parents, drug addicted parents, workaholic parents, parents who seemed the ordinary "Leave it to Beaver" parents. Some parents were university professors, some existed on welfare and had no occupation. The time the parents spent with their kids didn't seem to have anything to do with whether they worked outside the home or not, whether their job took them away for blocks of time or whether they came home every night; at least I didn't see those trends in those I interviewed.

Most of you were going to high school, some worked, usually at poorly-paying jobs, waitressing, dishwashing, acting. Bruce, the oldest at twenty-four, had a steady job in a warehouse. Jake worked two jobs plus his work as a drummer in a rock band. Some of you liked your jobs. Jake took satisfaction in his rock band; Robert with his acting and film production. Leslie enjoyed her volunteer work with a theater company, and Helen appreciated her job with the fast food restaurant.

I asked you about your living arrangements. Most of you lived at home. Sometimes you were still in high school and living at home and sometimes you lived at home because you couldn't afford to move out. Four were living in foster care but had emotional ties to their original family. Two of you were living with your boyfriend but still talked about your original family as the biggest influence on your life. Nine were living away from home in apartments but you still found your parents' opinion very important.

Mike told me about his struggles to be a part of his family but still to be independent and make his own decisions.

He was tall, dark, with black eyeliner to intensify his brown eyes. His black hair stood eight inches above his head in a punk hair style. He had one piece of curled hair that hung straight down between his eyes and stopped just above his mouth. For the first few minutes that free-swinging piece of hair distracted me. Then I stopped seeing it as we got more engrossed in our conversation. He wore a cross in his ear as well as other earrings, and black clothes—naturally. He had a wonderful sense of humor and very warm personality.

He fought with his parents constantly.

"My mother thinks we get along great but I don't think we get along at all. I couldn't talk to her. I couldn't tell her my problems. My dad's different—we don't get along at all. They think they're pro-talking, but they're not. My parents called me on Sunday [he moved out a month and a half prior to our conversation] to yell at me because of my report card. But I don't know. They were always pushing me and pushing me to get really high marks in school. I could if I really tried. But I never tried. I don't know. I never tried hard and they'd always get really upset with me and do things to punish me. Like I'm stuck in the middle of nowhere [the country] and the worst thing they can do is take the car. So they did. I'd lock myself in my room and I'd think about things like that. It just made no sense."

Me: If your parents were into talking, there had to be a reason why you wouldn't talk to them.

"They would tell their friends about it. That's one of the reasons I stopped talking to them. I couldn't trust them. My parents have this great imagination. They think that we are really, really close, yet I don't see that at all. I was close at one time to my mother, but never to my father. My father is the kind of guy, who

. . . I love baseball. Like I loved playing baseball when I was a kid. But being out on a farm where there are no kids around I was always by myself. My dad would come home on weekends and I'd go up to him and ask him if he would play with me and he'd say no, he wanted to sleep. He never played with me. Never. You know you always see the typical father on TV with his kids. I didn't understand why he wouldn't."

Me: Did you think it was your fault?

"Yes, exactly. We were never close but my parents always think we should talk to each other. Like, I should like unravel my heart? I can't. I refuse to, because I just don't trust them."

Helen did not have Mike's flamboyance nor his aggressive reaction to life. Helen was quiet, subdued. We met for coffee in a mall in Winnipeg. She was nineteen, worked as a shift manager at a fast-food restaurant, liked her job, thought she was appreciated there. She lived at home with her mother and father. She never felt that she belonged. "Ever since I've been little I've been sort of a loner. Not really having any friends. I never talk to my parents. I can't talk to my mom about anything." Her hope is to gradually increase her self-esteem until she can make her own choices and achieve more independence of mind. At the moment she feels flattened by the aggression in her family and in her social group.

It amazed me to hear how little intimacy you seemed to have in your families. Most of you seemed to exist in a world of superficial relationships where caring is shown by constant criticism. Parents demand better grades at school, different clothes, different friends, different music. The message to you is that whatever you are, it isn't good enough. Some parents told you that they criticized because they cared, but you didn't believe that. Few of you thought that your parents had odd ideas. Most of you thought that you were a second class kid. You did not feel you could sit down and tell your parents, or even one parent, what your problems were. You felt that would only invite more criticism.

What good is a counselor? Well, sometimes no good at all. But sometimes a counselor can make a great difference. Four of you were under psychiatric care and were managing on medication and counseling. More than half of you had tried talking to a counselor after your suicide attempt and had *not* been helped. You received such wonderful advice as "You just want attention." "How could you do this to your parents?" "Suicide is wrong and you shouldn't do it." None of which was news to you and none of which helped you one bit. A few, seven, got help from a counselor. You went to someone or your parents took you to someone or the hospital recommended someone, or you phoned a crisis center and asked for help and got help. Six of you never told anyone you had tried suicide before you told me, and you had never gone to anyone for help.

I asked you if you did call a crisis center or a distress center or a helpline. Most of you didn't. You didn't know about it and wouldn't have used it for reasons such as you thought it was too impersonal, you couldn't tell a stranger on the phone anything, you didn't think anyone would actually care, or it just wasn't something you thought of doing.

On my third interview the girl I was interviewing told me I should ask everyone whether they were sexually abused. I tried to remember to do that on all subsequent interviews. Did only sexually abused teens try suicide? Well, no. Six of you were sexually abused. If we take one in three as being the national average for women and one in five as the national average for men, that comes within our horrific national average.

You surprised me in telling me about physical abuse. There was a lot more of that than I expected. Most of you were hit by your parents, some of you until you were thirteen or so and others of you until you were fifteen or sixteen. What is really startling to me is that many of you accepted that as being your fault.

Beth, eighteen years old, pretty, thick, curly auburn hair. Her family lived in the wealthy district of Vancouver. Beth lived in an apartment with her boyfriend. She had furnished it with old, comfortable easy-chairs and sofas. Beth made coffee in her clean, tidy, almost artistically-arranged kitchen. She had a new kitten that purred at us, rubbed our ankles and messed on the floor. Beth put him outside.

She told me about her family.

"My father, he was, oh, he was scary. Very scary. Like we

would never talk back to him. And I suppose that's why we never talked. We were so afraid of saying something bad. But when I was about thirteen I started talking back. It was a mistake."

Me: What happened?

"He hit me. And I hit him back. Then he grabbed me and it was in the kitchen and he picked me up and put me on the counter and I kicked him and called him a bastard and he smacked me and threw me on the floor. I broke his chain that my mom gave him and I always felt bad.

"Funny, after my first attempt at suicide . . . just before that I had a boyfriend. It was my first boyfriend and my first lover. He'd smacked me around. I was used to it. My mother used to get really abusive, so I was used to it. And every so often he'd rape me, but I thought, well, this is my boyfriend, he just got aroused or something. And it was my fault. And before I went into the hospital I didn't realize how bad that made me feel. But they helped me see it there. Rape is rape. It doesn't matter if they're your boyfriend or not. I seem to attract men that hit me."

Bruce who had spent his growing-up years on the streets, told me: "I was never abused as a kid. I got my lickings like everyone else. And I should have gotten a hell of a lot more. Believe me I should have. I know I was really a hellraiser. I'd bite people and I got lickings for that. When I got older and I'd say to my mom, 'Oh, fuck off.' You know? She used to back hand me right across the face and say, 'Don't you ever say that to me again.' It got worse and worse when I was a kid. It seemed that there were arguments and fights all the time."

But Bruce doesn't see that he was abused, that the violence in his family caused the violence in his rebellion. He only sees that he "deserved" to be hit.

Tanya said she was never hit. "For a while, when I was three or four my dad used to smack my mom around. I feel that's sort of where my problems started. Like he lost control and then so did I. He never smacked me around. My sister got it, and my mom, but I never did. That's another thing. See, I was always his precious kid. And no matter what I did, I mean I'd get punished and I'd get sent to my room, but I never got hit. And I remember at the time I was never afraid of getting hit because I knew I never would, but now I wish someone would hit me. You know, I want someone to hit me. I want to be hurt, to sort of pay for the wrong things I do. I don't know if that's all related."

Leslie said, "They [her parents] used to hit us when we were younger and we had a lot of trouble with that. My sister ran away from everything."

Mona, eighteen, was independent, self-supporting, and was an enthusiastic, aggressive speaker. We met for lunch in a restaurant in down-town Vancouver.

"Like my jacket?" she said.

"Love it."

"Bought it with my own money."

"How did you get your clothes before?"

"Stole 'em."

She was happy both with her clothes and with "going straight". Mona had had a brush with the law on a stolen credit card charge and never wanted to be in the hands of the law again. Life was different for her now. She "had it together." She told me about her relationship with her dad. "If he gets mad he starts hitting. But he hasn't hit me in over a year and a half because I told him, 'If you hit me again, I'll charge you with abuse.' My head was ringing 'cause he'd hit me twice on the head and I wasn't going to have that any more. He'd hit me a lot before that. My mom didn't hit me though. She used to hit me when I was little. She'd say, 'You're a bad kid.' When I was fourteen I hit her back. I said, 'You're a bad mom.' So she said, 'This is where you take over, Daddy. You can take care of the brat from now on.'"

Amy, now baby-sitting in a suburb of Vancouver, didn't have much luck with her parents. "My dad's really violent. He loves to hit. He hits really well. My mom likes to scream. We used to fight pretty deadly me and my mom—fist-fight. It was pretty wicked. She'd hit me with whatever she had in her hand. If she was cooking, she'd hit me in the face with a spatula. She'd throw her dinner at me at the dinner table. One time she just about pushed me down the stairs. I got pretty fed up with it and I just close fisted her and knocked her right on her ass. It made me feel so good. Until my dad got home. And I got it."

Most of you suffered verbal abuse. You were yelled at, degraded, criticized, told you were incompetent, a loser, a misfit in the family. Sometimes you were told that your birth had wrecked the family, that your parents wished you'd leave. Under these conditions many of you had low self-esteem and considered suicide as a permanent way of leaving.

You tried suicide in many ways. You imitated movie stars and rock singers. You tried suicide in ways you heard about, read about or invented. Once you decided on suicide you saw many ways to do it.

Some of you wrote poetry to express your feelings. Not all of you, but some. When I read your poetry I could see the anger, the sadness, the depression you felt. Some of you still felt hopeless, useless. Some of you were past that and felt organized, ambitious, competent. It was only when you told me of the past that you remembered the pain that went with the confusion of the time.

I met thirty individuals. You weren't trying to represent anyone. There may be no one else in the world like you. You told me what your problems were, how you tried suicide and why. You felt the way some other teens feel. But I can't know that what you felt is typical. There may be many teens who feel the way you do and there may be few. There is no typical picture of a teenager ready to attempt suicide but there are signs and symptoms that may indicate when someone is thinking of it. (Chapter 7) "Teenage suicides" are not a type. You did share some common problems, but those problems didn't necessarily lead to suicide. They may have. It is dangerous, though, to think anyone can "tell". Anyone might try suicide, the girl beside you on the bus, your Chem lab partner, your best friend, yourself.

3

WHAT DOES YOUR FAMILY MEAN TO YOU?

I paint a pretty picture, for all the world to see
My smile is big n' brite, we all live happily
I don't want to continue, I feel so insecure
But my friends are always there, they help me to endure
We play this silly game, around the world we go
Are people here for real? or will I ever know?
I rub my knees n' elbows and get up one more time
I reach down for my mask, to complete my lonely crime
I sing their songs of longing and smile my life away
It doesn't get much better. I'm here, but not to stay.
— T.S.

I expected to find teenagers who had little to do with their parents, who were involved with their friends and spent little time at home. I thought that you'd tell me your parents were rather nice, but old, and remote from your lives.

You told me that your parents were more important to you than anyone else, that your parents influenced you more than anyone else. Even when you had left home and were happy, involved with a new loving relationship, you still looked on your parents as a strong influence. They mattered.

You looked on your relationships with your mother and father separately. If you knew both your parents, even if you were living with both, you thought of your relationship with each separately. You thought of your relationship with your mother as one thing and your relationship with your father as another. You didn't think of your parents as a team.

Somehow I had expected your relationship with your mother to be the all important one. I thought your mother's support and love, or lack of it, would be the most important thing in your life. But 27 out of 30 of you told me that you had difficulties with your father. You rated him anywhere from four to minus five on a scale of one to ten—ten was high. After the eleventh interview when I asked you how you rated your mother (on the scale of one to ten) I expected and received marks anywhere from four to nine. When I asked about your father I waited for a, "Oh, him. Maybe a 2." Even when your relationship with your mother wasn't good you still seemed to be bothered, disturbed, more by your poor relationship with your father than your poor relationship with your mother.

Why are dads so important? Most of you told me that you wanted your father's approval, that nothing you did was ever good enough for him. This feeling was offered by girls as well as boys. Girls were just as demoralized by their father's poor opinions as boys were. It helped all of you if your mother loved and supported you, but it didn't make up for the fact that your father didn't.

Some of you felt that you deserved this negative treatment from your father. You felt that you weren't much good, didn't do very well in school, didn't have many accomplishments. Some of you had grown past that belief and now felt that you were a "good" person, you did have talents and opportunities and you resented the pain your father had put you through, the doubts, the worries, the low self-esteem that you had lived under for years because, for a time when you were in your middle teens, you did believe your father. You were no good. Some of you achieved a tolerance for your father's attitude. Some of your fathers changed over time.

I had a very difficult time listening to you tell me how you were treated by your fathers. My father did not always understand me but he cared and he thought I was smart, likable, a little unpredictable, but, basically a nice kid. I was twenty years old before I realized that each of his children (six of us) thought he or she was Dad's favorite child. Why was it so hard for so many men to treat their children with respect? None of you "deserved" the treatment you got. Twenty-seven out of thirty of you could have used a different kind of paternal attention. It was hardest for me to listen to you blame yourself for your father's lack of love. "I know I'm not very special. I know I'm not what he wants." That was heart-breaking and I knew that nothing I could say would help.

I met Helen in a cafe in the center of a shopping mall. She was pale, self-effacing and soft spoken. She told me what life was like for her. "Ever since I've been little my father has always told me I was good for nothing. Ever since I was little. 'Stupid kid.' Stuff like that. From what I found out, I've had a few friends from my childhood try suicide, and they've gone through basically the same thing. I had one friend, her father called her a slut all her life. She finally ended up believing him that she was. I finally believed that I was actually worthless. I'm now trying to believe that maybe I'm not. But it's hard, after hearing my father for so many years."

What does society expect of fathers? Do men know how to be good fathers? Do they know how much they are needed? There has been such an emphasis on mothering, maybe your father needs to be told that he's important, that you need him. For most of you, telling your father something like that would be impossible. Your relationship is so poor that you think your father would see any sign of need from you as a weakness that he should discourage. Perhaps a counselor or someone your father respects could tell him, maybe another man, a business associate, a friend, his brother, his father, someone you could talk to, who could also talk to your father.

How do you develop intimacy with your father? We *are* talking about lack of intimacy here. So how do you get closer? How do you get his respect, love and encouragement?

You already know that every relationship is different, that there won't be any great rule that magically makes everything okay. But you might be able to make things better. Some of you have fathers who are alcoholics, some are workaholics, some are so withdrawn that you don't think it possible to ever reach them. I admit that such fathers are extremely hard to reach. The problem is, you probably aren't going to be happy until you figure out some kind of relationship that works.

Decide what you want. Maybe you want a warm, friendly father who is interested in what you do, who will listen to your problems and will share your enthusiasms. You want a father who will take you to the ball game, who will watch your skating practice, who will call you on the phone when you are away from home. You want someone who loves you.

Now. Some of you have excellent reasons for deciding that such an ideal relationship will not work in your case. If your father sexually molested you, you can't afford too much physical closeness. If he physically hits you, you can't afford to be around him when he's angry. If he drinks a lot, you don't want to be with him when he's drunk. These restrictions on your relationship are something you should think out. Even with restrictions, it is possible to work out a relationship that gives you some satisfaction.

Decide what kind of a person you are, what is important to you, what characteristics you have that you plan to keep, that you are not going to allow your parents to change. Assess what is valuable to you about yourself and let no one change that.

Then decide what you like about your father, what small change in your relationship you think you could achieve? There are some fathers with a great capacity for change, whose relationship with you has been good until now, but who are for some reason— a move, a job change, a divorce—temporarily emotionally far away from you. Those fathers might respond to straight talk. If you sit down with those fathers and explain your problem, what you want from them, how much you need them, they may make great efforts to improve the situation.

But for the rest of you, whose fathers have been withdrawing from you for years, who have hurtful patterns of behavior (yelling, constant criticism or sarcasm) straight talk is too hard. That doesn't mean *you* can't make changes. When you make changes in yourself, you'll find that makes changes in the people around you.

Don't aim too high. Pick one thing you want different. It can be as small a thing as getting your dad to say "Good morning" to you. Be positive about it. Don't get angry if he doesn't respond. Keep at it. This is a long-term project. It means increased happiness for the rest of your life. Get help with your efforts from a counselor (I know, I know, counselors aren't all good, but some are) or an uncle or some adult you trust. Find someone to talk to about what you are trying to do and take suggestions on how you can do it. Don't try to make great changes all at once. Look at this as a two or three year project and work at it steadily. Just the fact that you're working on it may make your situation seem more hopeful.

Your relationships with your fathers were very important, you told me. They influenced everything you did.

There were differences in how your fathers treated you but they seemed to separate themselves into a few patterns. Patterns in families are many and varied and teens may find their family has invented new ways of relating. Humans are different, families are different, so it isn't reasonable to think that everyone will fit into these patterns, but some will.

The Scapegoat

You were blamed for all the troubles in the family. If your parents quarrelled with each other, it was your fault, If your brother was in trouble at school, it was your fault. If there wasn't enough money in the house, it was your fault. While your family was busy blaming you they never looked at what was the real basis of the problem. Your father and mother continued to quarrel with each other and never looked at the real reason they were quarrelling. Every quarrel turned into a quarrel about you. You were used to being at fault and expected to be at fault. What happened after a while, was that you believed that you were "prone to trouble," that there was something about you that attracted trouble. Somehow you didn't know how to get along with people. You said and did all the wrong things naturally, you thought. You came to believe your family's estimation of you. This happened to a friend of mine. Her parents and her brothers and sisters got into the habit of blaming her. They were very nice people, fun loving, intelligent, friendly, hospitable but they got into a pattern of blame. This happens to very nice people. When she was fifteen she was in an accident and in the hospital and away from her family for eight months. In the hospital no one blamed her. She realized that she wasn't to blame for much of what went on around her. When she returned to her family she saw what they were doing and somehow, when she knew what was happening, it no longer had the same power over her. She stopped believing them. She just refused to accept their evaluation of her and she freed herself to grow in self-esteem.

The Loser

Your family decided that you were going nowhere. They made a collective decision that you wouldn't do well in school, you'd never get a job, you'd probably end up in jail, and there wasn't any future for you. They may have tolerated you at home but they had no expectation that you would bring them anything but trouble. As with the blaming, you believed it. Their expectations became self-fulfilling prophecies. Because your family thought you couldn't do anything, *you* didn't think you could. After all, if the people who knew you best and presumably loved you most, thought you were a loser, you thought they were probably right.

One way to get out of a pattern is to develop a life outside your family: at school, at a club, at your neighbor's house, at the sports arena, any place where you can spend a lot of time and accomplish something positive. That will make you realize that you have talents, that other people do recognize those talents, that other people like you and think you're great.

You may still need the support of your family. You may have to demand it. It sometimes takes years to develop enough confidence outside your home to be able to challenge your family. But if you don't challenge them, you may end up accepting their assessment. If you accept degradation, other people hand it out. Challenge them on little things. Don't let them put you down on little things. But you have to be strong to do this, and you may not feel strong at this time. Sometimes you have to live away from your family for years in order to be able to challenge them.

The Troublemaker

You were so handy for your family. They thought you caused trouble just by existing. Small things became big problems if you were involved. The family discussed you and your difficulties as if you weren't there. You provided the drama, the focus for the family. They never saw their contribution to the problems, their attitudes. They only saw your faults. It amazed you how ordinary, every-day living landed you in so much trouble. The family needed to rescue you from yourself all the time. You felt incompetent. They may have liked you but they didn't expect you to be able to look after yourself or to be able to solve your problems yourself. You always needed the family. They needed you to be helpless so they could be your helper.

The Perfectionist

Your parents expected you to be the perfect child. You managed to get good grades, meet their expectations. But, in your teen years, you had expectations of your own, your friends had expectations of you, your teachers had more expectations. You were used to pleasing your parents and you tried to please everyone. The stress became very great.

These family patterns are not unusual and they are easy to slide into. Some kids are not disturbed by them and the patterns play a minor role. But some kids are disturbed by them. Not all parents who are involved in these patterns are cruel and sadistic, although some are. Parents act out of habit. The goal is to try to change those habits so you don't suffer.

How do these kinds of family patterns make the teen feel?

Useless, incompetent, "bad," confused, rejected, unhappy and, *naturally*, rejected.

Leslie was the first teen I interviewed. She lived with her brother on the top floor of a house owned and occupied below by her parents. She was petite, lively and passionately committed to helping other teens who were thinking of suicide. She was working on a play about suicide and had been back to her high school to convince the guidance teacher to include suicide in class discussions. She taped our interview on her tape recorder as I taped it on mine.

She told me, "I used to think of my family as a wall. It was everyone against me. They used to blame me for something and I'd say nothing back. It's only recently that I stand up for myself. It used to hurt me a lot to think that these people are my family and they do this to me. But I guess they needed to get their anger out and they put it on me. If something went wrong it was always my fault. After a while I decided I might as well do rotten things because they blamed me anyway. I couldn't lose the respect I didn't have. I used to think highly of myself up to grade nine and then after that it was like . . . the shits. Sometimes I still think of my family as a wall because sometimes they still all gang up on me."

Bruce said, "I stayed in a house in downtown Vancouver. I can't remember the name of it. The correction officer there was really helpful. He said at any time if I needed him, if I felt like doing something stupid, to call him. He's someone I know I can trust. He's the only person in my whole life who ever worried about how I feel. Deep down inside. How I really feel. He made me realize that I could look after myself. Tell your parents to go to hell. Set yourself a pattern and follow it."

Janet lived in Calgary with her grandparents. She had been out camping with a girl friend for two days and missed our first appointment but was able to catch me before I left for the airport. We met at, of course, McDonald's. She talked about her grandparents.

"They weren't accepting me. I wasn't really a person. I was just something there. That's how I felt with them. I couldn't talk to them about anything. They were never really straight with me — like I was real trouble and had to be controlled."

Your parents' assessment is biased and may not be accurate. Your assessment of the relationship might be more real.

You told me that you had relationships with your brothers and sisters that ranged from very cold to very warm. However, your relationships with your brothers and sisters didn't seem to make much difference in how you felt about yourselves. You didn't necessarily believe your brothers' or sisters' opinions even if they were good. Now, this may not be true of all. I remember getting a lot of courage from my sister's belief in me. There must be others who did rely on a brother or sister. The problem seems to be that you didn't feel a lot of support from your brothers and sisters because you didn't see them as powerful in your life. They may be suffering from a difficult family pattern similar to yours or one quite different.

I asked you if anyone else in your family had tried suicide. No one who talked to me had lost a brother or sister to suicide but some knew their mother had tried it in the past. Some of you had lost a relative in death from other causes, when you were young. That is considered by some psychiatrists as significant in your own choice of suicide but you didn't tell me that. Leslie said it made a difference to her idea of life after death. You didn't tell me that thoughts of those relatives' deaths worried you. You didn't even tell me about the relative's death until I asked. So I can't know if a loss like that when you were young makes you more likely to try suicide.

Sometimes you felt that you fit in your family, that you were part of it, even when you didn't feel necessary to it. Many of you didn't feel needed and you didn't think anyone in the family would really miss you if you were no longer there. You thought you were in Helen's hole, the one she was trying to crawl out of. You felt that the ground could close over you and no one would notice you were gone.

When I asked you who you would talk to if you had thoughts about trying suicide again, no one said they'd talk to a family member; not parents, not brothers or sisters. It is important to remember that I only talked to thirty of you. Perhaps, if I had interviewed fifty teens, I would have found *someone* who would talk to a family member. Perhaps we need to expand our idea of "family" to include all the people who care for us and, in that "family," there will be someone who will listen.

4

WHAT DO YOUR FRIENDS MEAN TO YOU

The acts of defiance
There is no reliance
to what was then and
what is now.
Overcast greys biding down
They take the rejected
The street, the neglected
In the desolate night ghostly lies
Tears within trees of suspicious eyes
All the emotions, the dark sides
of life fought
Time deceives devotions, singles out our
wicked thoughts
Transformation, Termination, Situation, Animation
The games that are played to fuck up
our minds
The fearless monsters we think are our kind
The changes we take, the evil we love
The insane things we have all done
No one has won.

Mindgames.
— Diana

Friends are very important. You talked to your friends and you couldn't think of living without having friends. You seemed to need one intimate, close friend who accepted you, listened to your troubles and believed in you. A few of you had a friend like this, but, usually, your friends were not close friends.

Most of you would call someone a friend even though you didn't know her well and she didn't know you well. Friends like this may go to the same school, hang around the same mall, be members of the same clubs or sports teams.

Suzanne was fifteen years old, blond, looked seventeen. She invited me into her parents' split-level home in Calgary. We sat at the dining room table restricting our conversation to school subjects whenever her father or mother came into the kitchen, with apologies for disturbing us, and switching back to suicide when they left. Suzanne said she had not talked about suicide with her parents. I wondered what she told them I was doing in their house.

She told me that friends forced her into a cultural role that she wasn't sure she liked. "In the summer you can be yourself. [It was July when we were talking.] Like, I don't like hanging around my school friends in the summer. I already have a best friend. I have my out-of-school friends. I become myself really. When you're going to school it starts off okay in September. People say, 'Wow, have you ever changed.' Then you fall into the role. You fall into little social cliques. What's cool. What's in."

Me: So you adapt to survive in the school system?

(With surprise) "Yeah. I'm really easy to get along with at school. I make friends, not really friends, but acquaintances, really quick. But you have to learn how to act like no one, like an empty role, not real. I always find that you can't really say what you feel."

Me: Why?

"I'm always scared that people won't care. That you're just going to say something that really is bothering you and they'll just laugh at it. Because they've done that. They've just laughed. 'Don't be stupid!' You have to keep your opinions to yourself. You have to be able to laugh, be cool, flippant, don't care. You have to know how to make other people laugh, too.

"Last year I got put through it [ridiculed and I tried to explain to the people I thought were my friends, 'Listen, don't do that to me. It really *bothers* me.' And they wouldn't understand. 'Oh, it's just a joke. So what.' Like they can be cruel and then pretend they were funny."

Helen, nineteen, told me that she had only one friend during the period of her life when she was thinking about suicide, and before she tried it. "I had one friend, but I couldn't talk to her. She didn't understand. She was going through a rough time herself. She'd have asked me if I was crazy if I tried to tell her. So I just kept it to myself.

"I don't expect anything from people. I try not to expect anything because I've made friends before and I've trusted them and they've ended up hurting me. The way I feel, I can't trust anybody but myself.

"Friends don't talk about suicide. They know it's out there but they don't talk about it. It's like a taboo. A weakness."

Leslie lived in a suite on the top floor of her parents' house, but lived quite independent of her parents. She told me what it was like for her.

"I wish someone could have talked to me. I'd have paid money to have someone talk to me, like *look* at me, not at the picture I was painting for them. It [life] was too much of a game. Even now, some of my friends don't seem to realize how serious it was. Maybe they'll talk easier now, but suicide's too quiet a subject. Teenagers mention it. They say, 'Yeah, it's my parents . . . ' and this and that . . . but they don't say, 'It's because I don't feel loved.'

"When my friends talked about suicide they said, 'Let's all get really drunk and kill ourselves. That'll solve everything.' We'd go through the motions of getting really drunk and say, 'Let's do it.' But I don't know what made us stop. If they were going to jump I'd certainly have grabbed their hands and gone with them. We just didn't. We never talked about what we were feeling, just talked about life being lousy and we should get more drunk."

Some of you had friends that really cared. They may not have known how to talk to you about your problems or even how to listen but they were the ones who cared about you when no one else did.

One of the jobs of a teenager is to separate from the family. It's a preparation for independence and a family of one's own. Many teens transfer their affections from family to a friend, a boyfriend or a girl friend, and give that relationship the difficult task of satisfying the teen's need for affection, understanding and emotional support. Friends are *very* important in the teen years and they are *necessary* for most teens. It is usual for teens to form strong friendships outside the family and such friendships are an important part of moving away from the family.

In many cases, friends were your rescuers. After Leslie tried to hang herself, she stayed in her room and no one in her family worried about her.

"I stayed in my closet for three days. I thought that I wouldn't commit suicide, like suicide would be my fault. I'd just die of starvation, that would be natural. My brother's schedule was different from mine and he didn't know I was in the closet. I just stayed there.

"After three days, my girl friend came over and she found me. It just blew her mind. She was just crying. She got me out of the house. She pulled me out of the closet and she put me in her car and took me to a doctor. By then I was a mess.

"Anyway, my friend drove me to the doctor's and the doctor wanted to send me to a counselor but I ran out of there. I ran back to the car. I guess he tried to get my parents but I'm not sure if he ever did because they never said anything about it. My girl friend took me to some friends' place, Mike and Jason. She was really confused and crying and she said, 'She won't talk to me. Please. You've got to help her.' I was laughing and they were looking at me. I had already cut off the circulation to parts of my body and I was just skinny, you know and horrible. I just sat there. I was just sitting there still thinking childish things except there were people I kind of recognized. And then Jason gave me a hug. All of a sudden, I realized what was going on. I was looking at myself and my arms and everything and I was crying. They saved me really."

Leslie was the only one of the thirty who seemed to be influenced and helped by religion. She talked of finding her "salvation" and she considered her religious congregation a source of friends.

Many of you were rescued from the consequences of an overdose by your friend. Beth, eighteen now, sixteen at the time, told me that her friend helped her.

"My parents finally went away that weekend and they said, 'Okay, we're going to trust you. We're going away. You can stay here by yourself.' I said, 'Okay. You can trust me.' And I set out to really impress them because I didn't want to go goof off or anything. I don't know why it happened. All I know is I started drinking and I started taking some of my mom's pills and I don't remember half of it.

"We lived on the lake and I went traipsing around the lake for heaven's sake. And I remember parts of that walk but nothing else. All I know is what my friends told me. I guess I made all these phone calls to them. And the ambulance came to pick me up because my friend, my boyfriend at the time, was freaking out. And I said, 'No, I won't go.' So the ambulance couldn't take me. And my other friend, the boy I live with now, he came over and he's going, 'Mike, what are you doing sitting there crying on the steps?' And he said, 'Beth, she's in the house. She locked herself in the house and she's trying to kill herself.' And Jim goes, 'What?' And he tries the front door and it was locked and he walks around to the back door and it's wide open and he comes in and he convinces me to go back with the ambulance. I didn't even know what I was doing at the time. I wanted to write something down to my parents but it all hit me so quickly.

"My parents were up at Penticton when I went to the hospital. Then Jim sat and waited for me. The hospital had to have a relative sign so they called my grandparents. The next morning I went home to them. They had called my parents. I felt really lousy because my parents came home and I ruined their weekend."

Beth still sees that suicide attempt as an "inconvenience" to her parents.

Teresa used her friends as a family. "One of my friends' mother is really great. I can call her at any time, even four in the morning and she's wide awake and ready to listen. She's really great. I've gone to her a bit and we'll talk. I go over to their place for dinner once in a while."

Me: So you went out and found your own support system.

"Yep. I had to. It wasn't being offered anywhere. You pretty well have to go out and find someone. People aren't going to stand there with open arms and say, 'Come on here,' and all this. No one does this any more. Everyone's too afraid of getting involved.

"Nobody wants to get involved in someone else's problems. So Mrs. So-and-so has a problem kid. That's her problem not mine. That's the way people are. That's where a lot of people are going to be really screwed up. No friends. Nobody to care."

Sometimes it's the sudden absence of your best friend that leaves you vulnerable to suicide. Daniel's girl friend had troubles of her own at exactly the wrong time in Daniel's life.

I met Daniel, seventeen, on the wharf in Halifax. He was blond, broad shouldered and seemed confident. We sat in the sunshine and talked for so long that my face was sunburned for days. He was the youngest of five boys. His father deserted the family when Daniel was four, and his mother, a waitress, supported the family. Daniel had worked since he was thirteen while going to school and had managed to overcome a learning disability and stay on the academic program at school. He did not get along well with his older brothers but had a good relationship with his mother, none at all with his father.

At fifteen Daniel had been taking medication for depression and he knew the medication wasn't working.

Me: How did you know?

"How can I tell? You know how I can tell the most? Sleeping patterns. If I was happy, I could sleep. If I wasn't, I couldn't. If I was happy, I wanted to eat. If I wasn't, I didn't. So I called the doctor about three weeks later. So they took me down and they gave me this new blood test and they found that I didn't have enough medication and it wasn't working. For another two weeks they debated on what they were going to do and things at that point had become very disastrous.

"My girl friend's father is an alcoholic. He'd gotten the drift of where I had been and why I was there [in the hospital in the psychiatric ward]. His attitude was, 'He's not all there. He's sick. Don't be around him.' One night he began to beat her.

"She told me, 'Whatever he says or whatever he does to me, I won't turn my back on you.' She told me that one day, and the next night she said she couldn't see me any more because of her father. And I was feeling really, really terrible. The only thing that had really brought me around more than anything was her. I was happy with her. When she wasn't around I wasn't happy.

"I had this friend who was a drug pusher. So I went to him and I bought a bottle of amphetamines.

"At that point when I left the hospital the second time, it was the social worker and psychiatrist's recommendation that I not return home because of my grandmother [his grandmother constantly told him he was worthless], that it was not a good environment. My employer at the pizza shop told me I could live at her house. So I had moved in there. That was not a problem to me. I liked it there. There was no one at home. I took the amphetamines and lied down. I remember waking up three or four days later, after I'd been in a coma.

"My boss had come home to pick up some records or something like that and she usually checked to see where I was. She had knocked on the door and I didn't answer, so she opened the door and she couldn't wake me up so she called the ambulance.

"My girl friend . . . I hadn't seen her. I refused. I said, 'Just let me lie here and die.' I didn't eat. I had IV's. It was about three or four weeks before I decided to eat. Matter of fact, my girl friend *had* come back to see me. Her father had picked her up and thrown her out of the house. She, in turn, got hold of my mother and my mother gave her a place to stay. My girl friend had come down to see me and she told me what happened. Like she hadn't let me down. I just didn't know that. It kind of changed my attitude toward things again."

Daniel's will to live at that point depended on his relationship with his girlfriend. She was the only friend he felt he had, the only one who cared for him. And he could not stand, right then, to lose her. Another friend, his boss, saved him.

It is important for teens to have good, strong friendships. You told me that often it is very difficult to make friends with adults. That there is a great divider, the "them," adults on one side, and the "us," teens on the other.

Leslie had definite ideas on this. "When you're a teenager, you're not satisfied with anything. You're so uncomfortable. Everything is so new to you. You're right in the middle of young and old. You've got responsibilities, but nobody needs you.

"Society says to teenagers, 'Get lost for ten years. Come back when you have experience.'

"There's such a prejudice against teenagers. Like teenagers mean trouble. When you walk down the street people will cross the street. When people do that it makes me feel so low. When three teenagers walk down the street, people clutch their bags. And when you go and sit next to a person on the bus, they get up and move. My friends and I feel real bad about that. We don't forget that. We take this to heart. We generalize it, 'All adults this—and all adults that,' but that's so wrong because that's what they're doing to us."

Jake, eighteen, was a rock drummer in Toronto. He lived with his mother and visited at his father's apartment. He worked two jobs besides his drumming job. He told me. "No one seems to take teens seriously, including other teens. No one takes teenagers' pain seriously. They put it down. Other teens put it down. Negate it. Say, 'Oh, well, you only failed a grade, one grade. What's the big deal? I failed four. I mean what are you worried about?' Well, it doesn't matter if you did something worse, or better. This problem worries me. That's what no one seems to accept. That it worries me. It overwhelms me. Everything overwhelms me at this point. I think we don't care enough."

You told me that many times you tried to talk to an adult. Most of you saw adults as more capable of helping you when you were in trouble than your friends. Adults seemed more powerful, more able to change your lives. But often, adults did what Jake says they do, negate your pain, tell you it is nothing. Or, you tried to talk to them about a topic less scary than suicide and they didn't listen. So you were afraid to talk to them about something as serious as killing yourself.

Few of you were as independent as Daniel, who, in some ways is a street kid although he is cultured and educated and not in trouble with the law. He is so independent that he was able to move past the adults who tried to put him down, past the Helpline worker who dismissed him, to a good psychiatrist who did help him. Very few of you could persist until you found an adult who would help. It seems amazingly difficult for a teenager to find an adult who will listen. Many of you told me of feeling isolated, as if "being a teenager" means it is forbidden for adults to talk to you, or listen to you, or spend any time with you. I worked for twenty years as a public health nurse and I know that teens have trouble reaching the "helping system".

Many of you had good relationships with your families until you turned thirteen, then suddenly you had your own room, your own music, your own friends, your own timetable. Your family seldom bothered you, they seldom listened to you, you rarely did anything together. And you missed them. You felt lonely, rejected, un-real. You needed your parents to tell you you were okay. You needed them to tell you you belonged, were important, necessary. You needed them to be part of your life. Often you and your parents got into a pattern of reaction. You wanted to spend more time with your friends, so your parents reacted by spending less time with you. You reacted by never being around when they were home, so they reacted by criticizing the way you spent your time. You didn't tell them about school, so they didn't ask, so you thought they didn't care and your grades went down and they hassled you about your grades. Soon you lived a life separate from them, maybe in the same house but very separate. Yet you needed their attention, their concern, their love so that you could feel worthwhile and secure. But everything you did and everything your parents did seemed to drive you further apart leaving you feeling isolated and lonely. For many this was not a continual state. Things changed.

Some of you felt that you didn't fit into the world. You felt there were no jobs for you, no place for you. Society wasn't ready for you. No one was moving over to let you into the working world.

Suzanne tried to tell me how hard it was. "Teenagers are the most put-down, unsure . . . . Getting a job. You go into an interview room and I always feel so self-conscious. I look around and everyone else is in their twenties. Oh God. There's no possibility for me.

You know? Cause you haven't really had the experience. But you want the job. Like you're eager to do it and you're willing to learn. But they don't want that.

"I wish I was older. I wish I could be alone to live my own life, the way I want it. I could, but I'm too young. I can't get a job. I don't have the education. And even though I know I'm ready to do it, I can't. And so I have to put up with being a teenager, you know?"

Me: A second-class citizen?

"Yeah. You're not really important."

Me: Does anybody need you?

"Not really."

It was this feeling of isolation that drove so many of you to desperation. A good friend made you feel needed, loved and accepted. That feeling of acceptance was of vital importance.

5

HOW DO
YOU COPE?

At some time, for a few weeks or a few months or years, life was too hard. Everything was too difficult for you. Problem piled on top of problem on top of problem and there seemed no way of solving any of them. You were floundering in an ocean and there was no direction for you, but down. You tried to tell me about it.

Often, you told me, everything seemed too much because you had no help, no one who would hold you up when things were tough; you didn't feel that you could help yourself or you didn't know how to help yourself. I was impressed with your courage. You tried and tried to deal with the overwhelming problems. Often you managed for long periods but sometimes things got worse.

You looked for a respite, a time of peace, a place to hide. Sometimes you hid behind a stereotype. You dressed in a way that made others, including your parents, believe you to be a certain kind of person, a rocker, a punk, a loser. You hid behind that facade and thought your own thoughts and tried to deal with your problems. Others dealt with the picture you put forward, the stereotype, the cardboard image. "Why don't you get your hair cut?" "Green hair? That's ridiculous!" You successfully diverted their attention onto your appearance, a subject you could handle. And no one asked you how you felt.

You tried to deal with the ever increasing problems by escaping into booze and drugs. Bruce said, "I'd been feeling bad for years before the suicide attempt. I was drinking and getting high and I was thinking, 'Hey. This isn't me. I should be better.' I couldn't get it [schoolwork] in school. I felt like I was dumb. I felt like an outcast. I felt like Linus with the blanket. Everybody talks to him but nobody likes him. They see him walking down the street, they go, 'Hi, Linus,' and keep walking. That's how I felt."

Janet lived with her grandparents who were like a mother and father to her. She couldn't talk to them. The problems at home and at school got so unmanageable that she started, at fourteen, to drink. By sixteen she drank most of the time.

"I was scared of the future. I don't know, people say we're heading for another depression? And I don't want to live through that."

Me: What did it feel like back in that time. What did it feel like every day to be drunk?

"I was really hurting. I was a basket case. I'd go to school and I'd be shaking like a leaf, right? My relationship with my grandparents was zero in those days. My grades were bad, but they'd never been good. I told my grandparents my grades were my problem and I'd get what I wanted. They said, 'Well, we love you so much. We don't want to see your life fucked up. And all this stuff.' Well, it's my life. I'll do what I want. Get pregnant. Go on welfare. They said, 'We don't want to hear you talking like this.' But they were never really straight with me.

"Up to the time I was eighteen my life was just hell. I didn't like it. I didn't really have many friends. I don't know, I just wasn't happy. I suffered a lot emotionally. I had really little self-esteem, really little self-respect. I didn't think anybody liked me. I was picked on a lot."

Me: Why?

"I don't know. Maybe because I was fat or something. I think that was the main one. I went to school very day anticipating a rotten day. I didn't want to go. I was drinking all the time then.

"I can't think of anything that could have helped me then. My grandparents and I never had a listening relationship. I was like always put out of the way. Like when I was younger they were really close to me. I can remember my grandfather playing ball with me and everything. But that was it."

Me: So how did you learn to listen? When I talk, you listen. How did you learn that?

Janet laughed with surprise and then a little embarrassment. "Going to A.A. [Alcoholics Anonymous] meetings."

Not all of you used booze or drugs as an escape before you tried suicide. Some of you suffered a quiet anguish, withdrew into yourself, then tried to die.

Some of you dealt with all the overwhelming problems by pretending they weren't there. You lived every day as if the growing emotional problems didn't exist, and the growing practical problems of school grades, your job, a place to stay, didn't matter.

Beth told me that she hadn't realized that she was pretending so much until she went to a psychiatrist and got help understanding what was going on in her life. "I really had a neat trick. I just didn't think about it [problems]. When something happened to me I'd just store it away. I wouldn't think about it. Then, later, it was like a dam had burst and I had all these things piled up.

"I know the problems are there but I just kind of look at them through a window or something, not really look at them. I know they're there but I don't let the full impact of them hit me. I don't think about why things happen or what I'm going to do about it. I just store it away.

"Then, unfortunately, it all comes out at once and I get depressed. So I've tried to start working on things now as they happen. A lot of things with my family are still put away. They're there. I can sit here and talk about them as if they had happened to another person. I don't get into crying fits. But a lot of this came out afterwards and it was like, 'Oh, yeah. I remember this and I remember that.' All these different pieces of story finally fall together."

It seems to many of you that your parents are strong emotionally, that they manage *their* feelings and problems without great emotional upheaval. You then see yourself as weak, ineffectual, incapable. Why can't you handle your feelings as well as your parents? You think you *should* be able to deal with life, and you can't. Few of you get any help in learning how to handle feelings. Everyone uses escapes to get away from life occasionally. We watch television for escape, read books for escape, drink, listen to music, go to watch live drama, so that we can occupy our mind and our emotions without having to deal with life. Everyone does some or all of these things throughout their lives. Sometimes when life becomes too hard, we may even spend most of our days in escape. This is a great safety valve on our emotional lives. Problems come with the amount of time we spend escaping. Sometimes the escape becomes a life pattern. Some of you told me that just before your suicide attempt you day-dreamed all the time. You lived in a world of fantasy and seldom paid attention to what was going on around you. Some of you told me you went to school, came home and went to your bedroom where you listened to music for five hours. You did nothing but listen to music, or practice music, anything that kept you from thinking too much or feeling too much.

Sometimes these ways of coping helped a great deal. They took the emotional pressure off. You felt better because you were escaping pressure. But they didn't deal with your increasing need for love, attention and acceptance. You knew they didn't work because you tried them and you still wanted a bigger escape.

We have a basic need to love and be loved, a need for acceptance and we need to be secure in our parents' love.

Many of you tell me that, more than anything else, you need to be accepted. That you need to be accepted before you can change your behavior. Otherwise it isn't safe to change.

Suzanne said, "My parents put a lot of pressure on me, always nagging, nagging about my attitude, my personality, character. It was everything. They didn't like the way I was acting. I was going out too much. Everything. Everything I was doing was wrong. And maybe it was. But they should have told me in a different way. When school started again there was a lot of pressure from there. The teachers put pressure on me to do better in school and to change my attitude and my parents were fighting all the time and I needed attention. I needed some kind of different attention than what I was getting.

"I was popular. My friends were okay. But they didn't really know me. At that age, it's so important to be like everyone else that you don't really find out who you are. I didn't know who I was. I didn't know what I wanted. It was really tough."

Suzanne told me what many of you told me, that everything seemed to be too much and you couldn't decide what it was you should do and what would make life better. So you reacted to all the pressure in ways that you hoped would bring attention to your problems. You withdrew, to your room, to the crowd of kids you hung around with, to music, to booze. Or you hit back, in arguments with your parents, in arguments with your brothers and sisters, with sarcasm, yelling, loud music. Or you did what you knew your parents thought was wrong so they would notice you, got poor grades, came home drunk, left condoms around where they'd see them, shoplifted and got caught, wore clothes you thought they'd find offensive. Or you tried harder to be the perfect child, perfect grades, perfect clothes. You came in from dates on time, cleaned your room, and smiled, smiled, smiled. Life became confusing and painful.

Many found it impossible to deal with the pain. You knew that other teens dealt with loneliness, rejection, isolation from their families and you didn't understand why you couldn't. You felt different, less capable. Many of you were taught that you didn't have to deal with pain. You weren't expected to deal with pain. When you hurt yourself, your mother put a Band Aid on it. When you had a headache, she gave you a pain reliever. The principle of pain tolerance in most families was that if you had pain, someone would fix it; you weren't supposed to feel pain. No one sat down with you and told you that pain was part of living, that everyone has to deal with some pain, physical and emotional and that there are effective ways of doing that. No one sat down and said to you, when you have a physical pain you can deal with some of it by controlling your breathing, and showed you how. No one told you that when you had emotional pain you could deal with some of it by crying, some of it by writing it out, some of it by talking it out. No one helped you find your own ways of dealing with it.

So you tried to see what other people did; you watched your parents.

Janet watched her grandparents. "My grandmother would go into her bedroom and cry. That's how she dealt with it. My grandfather would yell so loud the whole house would shake. When I was a kid I was scared of him, but as I got older I thought, 'I can stand up to him.' And so we'd get to the point where we'd just be glaring at each other. Nobody knew who was going to make the first move and my grandmother would just be standing there like we were TNT going to go off any second." That angry reaction didn't help Janet cope with her emotional stress.

Robert's parents did not want to understand their problems. "They used to walk away. They'd argue and then say, 'I don't want to hear another word.' That's it. I was supposed to stop thinking. Just like that. Even though the emotions would be very intense. I think what hurt everyone more than anything else was just to stop and let everything stay at that level. They'd say, 'Don't say it. I don't want to hear another word about it.' That always got me. They'd say, 'Shut up.' And I'd say 'No.' And that would get them more angry with me."

Beth's dad didn't talk, and her mother said far too much. "My dad he doesn't talk about things. Apparently when I was young he didn't let me cry. Dad's one of those people that gets very uncomfortable when people cry. I don't know. All I know is he always scared me to death. My mom . . . well . . . before I went into the hospital [psychiatric ward] it was, 'I wish I'd never had you. You've ruined my life.' When my mother had me it was hard because she was just eighteen and she had to marry this man who she didn't want to marry. So they got a divorce and I've always been reminded of that. When I went into treatment I told the doctor this and my mom said, 'I never said that, Beth. I said I didn't want you before but then at five months I accepted you as my own.' I kind of went, 'Okay, well that's the impression you gave me.' Like my mother was brilliant and she was in school and she was going to do all these neat things. I always felt that I had to make it up to her. I had to prove that I was worth having."

Beth got a lot of attention from her grandparents but she doesn't think it was helpful. "My grandparents were always nice to me. Like my grandmother would buy me dresses and coats and she told me I could live with them anytime I wanted and all that. But I always felt she was nice to me only to bug my mother. I always felt like a tool she used against my mother. My mom says she's trying to steal me away."

Beth felt that no one was primarily interested in her.

Jake had a good relationship with his father but his mother and father were divorced and living separately. They had different ways of dealing with emotions. He saw different ways of handling life. "My mom yells and she doesn't stop. I yell back. I don't like being yelled at. Like I could understand if she yelled at me once but she goes on and on. She doesn't stop when I yell back but I can't just sit there and let her treat me like that. Sometimes I just take off, leave the house. But when I come back it's even worse like, 'How dare you leave?' And that kind of thing. I prefer it better just to get out.

"When my dad gets angry he won't yell at you. He'll still do things for you. My mom just yells and won't do anything. I like to get away from my mom when she's mad. Talking to her doesn't work. But with other people . . . I like . . . talk to them, work it out verbally. I say, 'Hey, you did this and I don't like it,' and kind of rationalize. It works better.

Teresa watched her parents handle emotions by denial. They pretended there were no problems. She was having a lot of trouble and her parents didn't think her problems were important. "The problems were a combination of things. Parents were probably the major thing. Friends were pressuring me to do things I didn't really want to do and I got suckered into doing a lot of things I didn't really want to do. And I felt like shit for doing them. But the pressures I got were unbelievable and my parents seemed to shrug that off.

"I wasn't doing what I wanted. And I hated me for doing what other people told me to do just because they said so. That's another thing my parents used all the time. 'Don't do this because we said so. What you want doesn't matter. You have to do it our way'."

Teresa's parents needed to see what Teresa did as important. They did not treat her cries for help as serious.

"I remember sitting there and methodically taking an Anacin and a Coke [Cola] and then an Anacin and then a sip of Coke. I sat there and watched myself get sick. It was bizarre. I sat on the chair and watched myself in the mirror. As my body started to get sick and it contracted and everything, I'd be moving and I'd watch it in the mirror. I had a sort of perverse sense of satisfaction. I thought, 'Actually, this might do it.' For about four or five months afterwards I had uncontrollable shaking. My nerves were shot.

"I was totally a nervous wreck. That was the last time I tried it [suicide] and I thought I'm not doing anything this way. I'm not accomplishing anything."

Me: But you wanted to suffer and you wanted your parents to see you suffer?

"Yeah. I wanted them to watch this but they weren't there. They were upstairs, sound asleep. Off in dreamland. I tried to make some noise. To maybe get them down there so they could see what was happening. But it didn't wake them up. I made a lot of noise without having them come and yell at me. They finally came down the next morning. I was supposed to be up already for school and my mom came in and said, 'How come you're not up.' And there was this bucket beside the bed and I had been throwing up all night. All over everything. I tried not to throw up but my body kept throwing things up.

"I was drained. And she said, 'What's the matter? Aren't you feeling good?' I didn't say anything. This had whacked out my hearing a bit too. It sounded as though she was standing about six feet away, or six miles away. I could hear her, just faintly, and I looked up and said, 'Mom?' and I couldn't see. I couldn't hear right. 'Mom, are you there?'

"She said, 'What the hell are you doing? You're supposed to be up for school already. Get going.'

"She looked around and saw the Anacin bottle on the dresser and the bottle of Coke spilled all over the carpet and she said, 'You got a headache?'

"I said, 'Mom, I've got a hell of a lot more than a headache,' and I just laid back down.

"She said, 'What did you do?'

"I wasn't about to tell her I tried to kill myself. I just lay there. She started yelling and screaming and calling me a stupid kid and what was I trying to prove?

"I just gave up trying to talk to her and rolled over and said, 'Leave me alone. Get the hell out of here.' I tried to go to sleep.

Then my dad came in. Like Mom must have gone upstairs and said, 'Come here, John. Look at this one.'

"He came in and said 'God! Kids!' and he walked out.

"And I lay there and cried and cried. And they never came in again and they never said anything. It didn't do a damn thing. It didn't matter what I did." Teresa's parents denied her problems even when they could *see* the problem. They pretended that nothing serious was wrong.

Most of you learn from your families, from your teachers and from your experience, to think of emotions as "bad." Anger, fear and sadness are bad. Emotions are something to be feared, suppressed, denied. Suzanne found that she wasn't supposed to be anything but happy. "If you're in a family it's always that you have to be so happy! My mom always demands . . . [happiness]. If I'm really depressed and I'm walking around the house sad, she says, 'What's wrong with you? Why are you being such a bitch?' It's like I want to say, 'Leave me alone.' But we're supposed to make her happy. We have to. She has to stop and make us happy. No one's allowed to be unhappy around her. I knew I was in trouble with my parents when my attitude was mopey so I have to cover up those feelings. I always felt that. I couldn't be unhappy, I couldn't be hurt. I couldn't be sad. And you feel everyone else is like that, hiding things."

Suzanne saw emotions as risky. "I don't show my mother my emotions. I either tell them to Tanya [her girl friend] or call my brother, or cry and think for a while. And once I get myself together I can tell my mom about it. She can tell when I'm sad or whatever but I've got control over it."

Me: Would it be disastrous for you to lose control in front of your mother or dad?

"Yeah."

Me: Why?

"Then I'd have to depend on them. I couldn't depend on them before. I always had to depend on myself. So I wouldn't really know how they would take it. I'm afraid of my temper. I kind of have to hold it down and it's bottled. Sometimes I have to be alone to let it explode. Right? Dispense, sort of. I think emotions aren't socially acceptable.

"Even if you're too happy, it's not acceptable. Then everyone thinks you're spinny. If you're going out somewhere, and you're waiting at the bus stop and you're dancing around, people are watching you. And you feel so . . . . You think, 'What am I doing? I know I'm acting weird but this is the way I feel.' That's not socially acceptable."

Me: Being happy is suspect?

"Yeah. You're a teenager. If you're happy, you must be on drugs."

So many of you are afraid to risk showing your emotions to your parents. Often, you have good reason for being afraid. In some cases your parents ridiculed you, or used what you told them against you at another time, told their friends, put you down. You've experienced this in the past, and you think it will happen again. Telling your parents about your problems has only made more trouble in the past. You couldn't afford to tell them how you felt. But, because you needed help with your feelings and because you couldn't talk to your parents about this and didn't know where to go for help, you felt helpless. You didn't understand how important it was for you to get help.

Some of you lived in an environment where you were ridiculed and belittled. No one showed you how to cope. No one expected that you would cope well. After you reached about thirteen you started to see how your family interacted. You started to see patterns. You started to understand that you were rejected. Up to this point you had tried to pretend to yourself that deep down your parents truly loved you. After thirteen you were more realistic, perhaps more capable of coping with the knowledge that their love was not enough for you. They may have loved you but were inept. They may have loved you but had so many problems themselves they couldn't help you with yours. They may have loved you, but were so emotionally upset with each other that they didn't see your problems or didn't see how serious your problems were. Or they just may not have loved you.

After about thirteen you started to see how your parents used you. You did not want to be used, as a bouncing ball between them, as a scapegoat for all the blame in the family, as a focus for fights.

You turned away and that caused changes in your family, caused friction. When you got older you started to create a power base of your own and that did not fit with your family's idea of you.

Many of you needed to be shown how to deal with problems. You needed to be shown what's expected of you and where you fit into your family and into your social group. You needed to have your mistakes accepted as a way of learning and not evidence of basic incompetence, or evil. Being allowed to fail is a way of learning. When you were five your parents taught you how to tie your shoes. They didn't turn you over to social welfare because you couldn't tie a knot the first time you tried. Yet, when you hit thirteen some parents seemed to think you should suddenly know how to act in all situations. In some families no one took time to help you with your mistakes. Of course, you were going to make mistakes. How could you avoid them unless you spent all day in your room listening to music and avoiding life? Most of you didn't want to leave your parents and strike out in life making one mistake after another. You just wanted the freedom to try things your way and come back home and talk about it, figure things out and go out and try life again. You wanted a home base, a support system, some kind of acceptance of you as you are.

6

WHAT MADE
LIFE HARD

I asked all of you what happened in your life to make suicide look like an option to you. It was hard for me to imagine why suicide would look good. I didn't instinctively understand. I had to be told. You had a lot to say.

Suzanne said, "The psychiatrist figures that with everything . . . I just couldn't take myself any more. The first time they figured I was rebelling and it was a call for help. I needed to talk to someone. But the second time, I just couldn't cope. I was really letting my parents down and myself down and the world down.

"The first time I wrote three poems before I did anything and I showed them to my mother. She thought they were very nice. They were interesting. She tried to analyze them herself. Some of them were about death. Most of them were analogics like the sun slipping below the horizon, broken glass . . . My mom thought they were about my boyfriend leaving me, but they weren't."

Me: How did you feel before you tried suicide?

"Before? You know when you're going to cry and you get a lump in your throat. Well, it's just like the lump is your whole body. You're always tense inside and you don't trust yourself."

Me: How long were you depressed?

"It's hard to say the first time because I'd never had much happiness before that with my family. It was at least a month but I'd never been really happy so maybe it was years.

"I thought death would be like falling asleep. There'd be nothing. But I wouldn't have to put up with what was going on any more. I wouldn't have to keep hurting people and I wouldn't have to keep hurting inside. That's all I knew. I didn't think I was going to go to heaven or anything. I was happy with that. Going to sleep was okay. Then I wouldn't have to do anything. People wouldn't expect so much of me. I wouldn't expect so much of myself. I could stop going around pretending I was happy all the time, doing what everyone else wanted. I'd just be myself. It would just be like black. No dreams. Nothing. I wouldn't have to do anything or see anyone. I never felt that I'd float over my body, have my soul set free or anything. No. Just black.

"I never thought I'd fail the suicide. It was difficult."

Leslie, eighteen now and enthusiastic, energetic and keen to have me help other teens, told me what life had been like for her. "I used to shoplift when I was twelve. We were better off then [parents had more money] and I used to have money in my purse but I stole things I didn't need. I knew I was going to get caught. And I wanted to. I went home and got into trouble and that was it. I went home and it was like, 'You're bad. You're bad. You've destroyed our family name.' The family name! That was the most important thing. I couldn't believe it. I didn't do it [shoplift] after twelve because I thought, 'Well, that isn't the way to go. What is the way to go? How do you cry for help around here?' So I used to get caught at a lot of things at home. I used to bring booze home and leave it in obvious places and I'd get caught and they'd say, 'You're even worse than I thought. I've lost all respect for you.' And I said, 'That's okay. I've lost all respect for you too. Can we talk?'"

Leslie tried many ways to get attention from her parents and met with constant rejection. A few months ago everything became too much. She had an interview with the school counselor in the afternoon. The counselor criticized her and didn't help her. She went home. "My boyfriend called and said it was all over. I hung up the phone and walked into my bedroom. It was like there was so much pain I had to get away from it. Like I thought I was dead anyway, my mind was dead, my body might as well be dead too. I hung myself, but the cord broke. So I wasn't dead. And it was like God didn't want me either. No one wanted me. My mother had told me that like my grandma and grandpa died within a month of each other when I was about five and my mother said it was better for grandma. Like there was no more pain for her. She was with God. She was in heaven. I thought it would be good for me . . . And then not even God wanted me. I stayed in my closet for three days.

"My only other option [than suicide] was to talk to someone and I wasn't good at that at that time. There was no way that I could just release it all without help. There was no way I could do that after seventeen years. I tried the counselor and that didn't work. I couldn't talk to my parents. I wrote in my diary. To go see a psychiatrist meant lots of money [not necessarily, but Leslie thought it cost money], and people saying 'Why do you want to go see a psych?' 'Are you crazy? What's wrong with you?' I would have loved to go see a psychiatrist, if I had the money and the guts.

"I thought about the Crisis Centre once but looking for the phone number was . . . you know, too much. I called Zenith 1234 but I think that was for Child Abuse. That was the only number I knew because I remembered it from the television commercials. So I phoned them and they said, 'What area are you?' And I said, 'Vancouver.' And they said, 'Can you hold on a minute?' and that blew me away. Hold on a minute? I was crying when I was on the phone. I hung up.

"After I didn't complete suicide that must have been the lowest point. And then things got better. I started to realize why I do things, where all my feelings spawn from. I started to feel comfortable with my own emotions. Then I could start to relate to other people. I started to get my self confidence back. It's only been four months. I've changed a lot in four months. I think so differently. The thing is, I haven't forgotten what I've done. I don't wish to forget because I want to learn from it. But when I look back I can't believe that things could get so bad. I'd like other people to know that things can get bad. When it does get that bad, go get somebody to listen to you, to talk to. I don't think I could ever turn my back on anybody now. Not since I've been there."

So many of you told me how events piled up one on another

until you had absolutely no idea how to deal with them. You saw nowhere to go, no one to talk to.

Bruce tried to cope with increasing problems when he was very young. He tried suicide first when he was thirteen. "I came home and my dad wanted to see me. He wanted to take me to Kamloops and my mom didn't want me to go. My mom was living with this guy. I was feeling pretty shitty. My mom always had lots of pills hanging around. Pills were my favorite things. I loved to take pills. They blanked you out.

"I came up from downstairs in our house. I'd taken lots of pills and I grabbed a pair of scissors and tried to stab myself. My sister twisted my arm and knocked me down the stairs. The ambulance came and they took me to hospital. They pumped my stomach and kept me overnight. I didn't tell anyone about the pills but my sister had seen all the pill bottles lying around. They didn't really do anything in the hospital. They gave me a medication that made me throw up. The doctor said, 'Why did you do this?' And I said, 'No reason.' Four hours later my mother and her boyfriend picked me up and took me home. That was about it.

"I think that I was really asking for help. I've been to quite a few doctors, psychiatrists, now to find out what was going on. I think at that time I was trying to get my point across. 'Listen, you guys. I don't want any more of this shit. I don't want it any more!' Finally I just said, to my parents, 'Piss off. You guys fight on your own. I'm butting out.'

"When I tried suicide I thought the problems would go away. There would be no problems. If you don't like something, you get rid of it, right? There'd be nothing more to cause pain. 'You guys [his parents] won't go away so I will. I tried to run away from you and live my own life [on the streets] but you wouldn't let me. Why do you keep bringing me back to this place? I don't want to be here.' All the time my parents were dragging me in the front door, I was saying, 'Don't do this. I don't want to be here. Let me go.' I was there, how long? four hours, five hours? and then I was out the back and on my way again.

"At thirteen I thought of suicide as 'going away,' not really dying. But after a while I came to respect death.

"But I tried suicide again. I figured this [living on the streets, on booze and drugs] was going to be my life. And if this was it, I didn't want it. So I took a Coke can and ripped it in half and cut my wrists. Maybe I didn't want to die. Maybe I just wanted to talk to somebody. That's when I went to S . . . Centre [Juvenile Detention Center]. The RCMP took me to the hospital. They fixed me up and left me in a padded cell for the night.

"Later, when I was in jail, I come to grips with reality. I seen somebody die. The guy in the next cell killed himself and I seen them take him out. I thought, 'When I die that's probably what I'm going to look like.' I seen him lying there and he wasn't moving. He was just lying there and his eyes were open and he wasn't moving. He looked peaceful and all unconcerned you know.

"I realized that you can't get up from this and walk away. So suicide went out of my head."

Suzanne was twelve when she first tried suicide. "Before, I was having a lot of problems with my parents. I didn't feel like I belonged in my family. I was so different from everyone else. That's why I was so glad to go on the holiday with my friend and her parents. But I got into trouble on that holiday. I lost my virginity. I lost all my pride. I wasn't sexually assaulted, I co-operated, but I wasn't mentally ready for it. I mean the guy didn't give a shit. It was a one-night stand for him. My virginity was the only thing I really had left and I lost it; and I was twelve. [Suzanne took an overdose, 38 Tylenol. Her friend didn't want her to die and persuaded her parents to take Suzanne to the hospital. Suzanne's parents never did know about this attempt.]

"Once you try suicide then you think about it. It's easier to do the next time. (She spoke softly, slowly, remembering what it was like.) People who haven't tried it can think. But thinking and doing are different things.

"So it was really easy for me to try it again. Like a habit . . . like, 'Try it, see if it works.' But I didn't really want it to work. I just wanted somebody to listen. So I just was thinking and thinking and I OD'd and my last thought was what if Dad comes home and I'm not dead yet he'll have to to stop it. He came home and he stopped it. I haven't tried it since. The thought's there when something happens. People can do it [attempt suicide] over the dumbest things but to them it's most important.

"I still wanted to try suicide. I didn't know what to do. Like should I leave a note? I just wanted to be be alone. Running away occurred to me. But I didn't do that.

"Now it's easier to deal with my feelings. One time I got out the razor blade and I sat there and I wanted to do it. But I couldn't. I felt like I could always make life better. Like I survived before. Maybe I can do better this time. You sure don't like yourself when you're thinking about suicide. And you think that other people don't like you."

Me: Do you think about whether your parents will miss you when you're gone?

"You don't think about that. Just don't think about that. I wrote poems and they were really sad. I still had one girl friend who really cared about me but no one else cared. I had a boyfriend but he didn't really care about me. I'd go to school and then come back to my room but I kind of wanted it that way, you know?

"Once you have the idea in your head, it's something you can't get out. When you see a bottle of pills you think, 'Why don't you take them? It'll all be over. It'll all vanish.'

"I feel like I can handle myself better now. Like I can handle my emotions. I can deal with the thought of suicide. I can sit there with a razor blade in my hand for an hour, just thinking and come to the conclusion that, well maybe I should just wait and see what happens. See if things will get better."

Teresa looked at death a little differently.

"I tried the razor blade about four times. Then a friend got me her grandpa's nitroglycerine pills. That just about did it. I did that [tried nitroglycerine tablets] at a party and they took me to the hospital. My mother never found out about it. I wouldn't give them my name. I had no ID. And I wouldn't tell anybody at the hospital who I was. So they just cleared up the nitroglycerine problem and sent me on my way.

"I tried to jump in front of a car once but I'm scared of cars and I couldn't do it. A big semi came along and it would have been perfect, but I couldn't do it."

Me: Did you think about how the driver would feel?

"No, not at all. I never thought about the effect on anybody else, really.

"I thought about what it would be like after I died. My parents would be sobbing at the funeral saying, 'We should have talked to her when we had the chance. Now it's too late.' I'd be sitting there laughing and saying, 'I told you so.' Not really watching the funeral but an 'out of body' experience."

Me: You didn't see death as final?

"No it didn't really strike me that once I'm dead, I'm not coming back. It didn't strike me as that final. It would be like I could be watching the funeral and I could be laughing at it."

Me: When did you see death as final?

"When I tried the Anacin and Coke. I was hoping to God it was going to be final so I could get out of this life. I was hoping it was going to be slow and painful too so I could say, 'Look Mom and Dad. Watch me suffer. There's nothing you can do about it.'

"When I woke up the next morning it was, 'Shit! It didn't work!' I blamed myself because it didn't work. Which was stupid.

"I was furious with myself for weeks because I didn't do it right. I was a failure that way too. I couldn't even kill myself properly. What can I do right? I can't even kill myself. By that time, [she was seventeen] death was definitely lights out.

"After the Anacin and Coke time I realized that I wasn't getting anywhere trying suicide.

"I decided I was alone. My parents didn't give a damn about what I was doing. They didn't give a damn about what I said. I was only a burden to them. I wish I had succeeded at suicide so I could take the burden off their shoulders. That's the way I felt. And I really wished it had worked.

"But I also thought, 'I'm not killing myself instantly. I'm killing myself slowly.' I didn't want to do that.

"I decided that if I really was a pain in the ass to them [parents] I'd work for myself. And everything picked up after that. I started working at everything. My grades picked up, my appearance picked up. I dropped about sixty-five pounds. Everything just changed then."

Amy had been kicked out of the house when she was about fourteen. She had to deal with a lot of rejection from her parents. Suicide looked better to her than the life she was living. "I took a major dose of 292's and 222's and a bottle pain relievers. I don't know what they were. I would have died except my boyfriend's brother came in. I was getting pretty buzzed by the time I finished all this. He freaked out and brought his mom. They made me throw up.

"I wouldn't go to the hospital. They made me drink, I swear, a dozen of those big jugs of water and it made me sick.

"There have been so many different times and so many different ways I've tried suicide. I've tried doing my wrists and I guess I didn't do it right. Obviously, I didn't do it right. I've tried hanging myself and I couldn't find anything strong enough to hold me. I tried tying a shoe lace around my neck. From the age of thirteen to about seventeen I tried all kinds of things. I tried to OD and all I did was make a mess and embarrass myself.

"I got picked up once by some Mormons and I freaked them so badly. They really cared. They made me feel a lot better. I guess from that point on whenever I got myself into a desperate situation I realized that suicide is useless. I guess I don't have the guts to do it right or something. Or there are too many people around to stop me. All I end up doing is making a mess, making a fool of myself, making people angry at me.

"And I know now that things always get better." Amy felt that since she had managed to live through such a terrible life, she was strong enough now to deal with anything that came her way. At eighteen she now has a strong love for her boyfriend and a network of adult friends. She feel she belongs in this world and she is worthwhile. She feels like a different person than her seventeen-year-old former self.

Daniel, seventeen, is independent, used to relying on himself. "I became very withdrawn. I stopped eating. I wasn't sleeping. I was having bad headaches all the time. When I did sleep I was having nightmares. I was getting very depressed. I didn't care about school. I didn't care about my friends. I didn't care about anything. I was withdrawn. I went back to one of my teachers from junior high, Mr. R., and he said, 'You know I think you're depressed. I want you to get a' hold of this doctor.' I had the name but I didn't call and then I got kind of desperate so I called the Help Line and that didn't do anything. So I called the number he'd given me and they said they could give me an appointment in six weeks. The thing was, I couldn't wait six weeks. I couldn't wait six weeks at all. So I went to slashing my wrists. The problem was that the kitchen knives weren't very sharp. If I'd had one of the knives I used at work [pizza joint] I wouldn't have had a problem at all.

"I was home alone. I planned it about a week ahead of time. I'd been thinking of suicide for about a week. I'd decided that there was no way I wanted to come out of this. There was no way I wanted to live my life like this. I didn't really know what was going on. Then it didn't work. And I felt worse.

"It was even worse. I was trying to think how I could do it. My teacher, Mr. R., kept phoning me. Finally one day he said, 'Go to the doctor.'

"Before I did though, something more happened. What happened that night, we received word that my brother had died. He'd blown up in a tank accident in Lahr, Germany. He was the member of my family that I was closest to. I called again to the doctor and told them 'I can't wait that long [six weeks].' So they gave me an appointment for that week. They gave me an appointment with the staff psychiatrist and in a matter of two hours I was in the hospital before my mother even knew."

Daniel impressed me very much. He was certainly alone in that he had no strong social support system. And he managed to get psychiatric care from that system. His mother did love him. He was in no doubt of that. His father did not. He was in no doubt of that either.

Robert, nineteen, told me about his suicide attempts.

Me: The first couple of times you tried suicide, did you think death was final?

"Not really. I thought I'd just go somewhere else. What I did next [first time he OD'd] I threatened to slash my wrists. I was trying everything. And then it gets even better because I figured no one was taking me seriously, I couldn't do anything so I got into stunt training. I figured if I died there I was getting paid for it and it wouldn't matter if I died there. I had no one else to worry about. It was a different type of suicide. I was by myself. I lived on the edges of buildings. It's scary because it's a long way down. But it doesn't really bother you because you figure, 'Well, okay, if I die, well, it's my time. It's one way of getting out of this thing [life].'

"Doing the stunts, well, it didn't bother me but it bothered my friends. It scared them to death that I was so casual about it. I did it for kicks then. Walk on the edge of a building, on the outside of a bridge. It was a game with me then, flirting with death. When we did a stunt off a building we were supposed to have a wire holding us. I didn't use a wire. It was scary. I remember one time I wasn't really thinking about it and I almost slipped showing somebody something. And I remember how scared I was. It kind of snapped my mind out of it.

"It wasn't that I decided death was final right then. It was more getting all my act together. There was no need to die now. I could live my own life now. It really doesn't bother me now what other people do. I can make it on my own. I think it's a phase that people go through. That eventually, if they come close to death, without actually dying, especially when they aren't meaning to die, and they know it, they'll snap out of it, teasing death like that. Life only matters if you're leaving someone behind. If you don't have anything, dying doesn't really matter too much." Yet Robert had decided that life was good now and he wanted me to tell other kids to hold onto it.

Tanya talked about trying to die and wanting to die and then suddenly talked about truly *not* wanting to die. That seems like a contradiction, but many of you felt that you wanted to die at the same time you wanted to live.

Me: (Talking with Tanya) Why did you think suicide was the only thing that would work for you?

"Because there was no one for me. And if there wasn't anybody then I couldn't live here all by myself.

"I didn't want to run away because I didn't want to hurt my parents because they'd never done anything to me." (Yet Tanya had told me of parents that were cool to almost indifference, who had high expectations of her, of a father who abused her mother. Her life had not been happy.)

Me: But wouldn't suicide hurt them?

"I wasn't planning to die."

Mike, my friend in Toronto with the exaggerated punk haircut and the great sense of humor, told me about his suicide attempt.

"I took an overdose of sleeping pills. I was baby-sitting my sister's kid. The kid, who was two, was in bed. I took the pills and felt relief. I was hoping that it would finally be over. That's the way I wanted to go. Just fall asleep. I'd wanted to do it for so long and then I finally did it. I thought about killing myself for about a year and a half.

"Every time I had a fight with my parents I'd think about suicide. Or if something bad happened at school, I'd be lying in my bedroom listening to music and I'd think about it.

"My sister came home early. She rushed me to the hospital and they made me throw up. But I didn't throw it all up so they pumped my stomach. It's gross. Thankfully, my parents didn't ever know about his. My sister kept her mouth shut. Like I asked her not to tell. My sister and I are very close. We have no secrets from each other.

"I made a deal with her that I wouldn't try it again if she didn't tell our parents.

"The hospital psychiatrist saw me one day. He came in and talked about it but I never saw him again. He didn't do anything. He didn't help me with my suicidal tendencies.

"I had thought about all the reasons why I needed to kill myself. I'd thought them all out in my head. I thought I had to do it because of all the things that were going on. I just didn't think anything was going to get better. It was either that or leave home and that didn't seem like it would help. It would just cause more problems."

Me: Why isn't running away an option?

"It would just cause new problems. You'd have to get a place to stay and all that.

"Just before I tried suicide my girl friend's father and little brother were killed in a car accident. Her whole family leaned on me. Her mother and brother. I was seventeen. Her mother, well, my girl friend had been telling her mother that her and I were going to get married in May so her mother thought we were engaged and that explained why she leaned on me. She thought it was appropriate. I was out of town at my sister's when this happened and I flew to Toronto at six in the morning, the first flight. I stayed with my girl friend for a while at the hospital. The thing that really worried me is that I'd never seen a dead body before, right? But I went to the wake and I saw them, both of them, the father and the child, lying there. And I couldn't cry. I didn't have any kind of inclination whatsoever to cry and that really worried me. It was so sad. I loved them both so much especially the child. He was two years old. His second birthday was just two weeks past. He was such a sweetheart."

Me: The abortion [his girl friend's, his baby] was first, so that this was like three deaths?

"Exactly.

"My girl friend was leaning on me a lot because her parents had just got separated." Mike looked up suddenly. "This sounds like a soap opera."

Me: Was there anything else?

"Probably.

"I went back to my sister's and the day I tried suicide I put the baby to bed at eight and then I took the pills and after I did it I was talking to a friend on the phone. He might have called my sister. He might have known I had taken something. Maybe that's why she came home early. It was the week after that had happened to my girl friend's father and brother. It was really my first chance to be alone and to try something. When I had been home with my parents I had thought I didn't really want to go that way. I had another way I preferred. You know, I'd planned it out. Get in the garage and turn the car on. That way you just fall sleep. It's a lot easier and less painful. But my sister didn't have a garage so I had to go with my second choice. Pills.

"When I tried suicide, yeah, I thought death was final. I don't believe in life after death. Yeah. I thought it was final. I just thought it would be better to die. I didn't expect to survive. I hoped not to.

"Somebody should have listened to me and maybe just talked to me like a good friend or something. Helped me out."

Whenever you told me about why you tried suicide it seemed that whatever happened to lead up to the decision, either a long decision taken over weeks or a quick, impulsive decision taken in minutes, came on top of months, sometimes years of problems at home. Of course, that may not be true for all. Some may truly have a sudden, compelling yearning for suicide.

Janet told me, "I stole some money at school, I was twelve. I got suspended. My grandmother said, 'Don't think about running away because the police will catch you.' I didn't want to go through what I was going to have to go through with the principal and everything so I just took some pills. And nothing happened. I thought they were strong. I threw up quite a bit. But nothing happened.

"I don't think anyone knew. I told my girl friend a long time after."

Janet tried suicide again at seventeen.

Me: Why was suicide an option?

"I wouldn't be here to face life, right? I'd be gone. I wouldn't have to cope. I thought of death as just not being here."

Me: What do you wish would have happened when you tried suicide?

"I wish I'd have died." Four of you answered this question by telling me that. But when I asked Janet what would change her mind if she was thinking of suicide right now, she said, "Just a little light at the end of the tunnel. Even a little light."

If she could think that life would get better, if she had some hope, then she would try to cope.

7

WHAT NEEDS
TO CHANGE
IN YOUR LIFE

She sits in the corner, her back to the wall
Students that whisper say nothing at all
She plays with her pencil, her fingers, her hair
The center of gossip in quiet despair
The teacher prejudges by where the girl sits
In the back by the window, she never quite fits
The teacher looks down with critical eyes
The girl smiles back, her face telling lies
The teacher tries hard to know the girl's thoughts
But never quite knows how far she is lost
Confused to the point where eternity ends
She doesn't need critics, she simply needs friends.
— T.S.

Because I only talked to thirty of you I cannot come to sweeping conclusions about what all Canadian teenagers felt, or North American teenagers. I can only report what thirty of you think and feel. You certainly weren't all the same. Many different types of people consider suicide. It seemed reasonable to assume that many people, if the circumstances are severe enough, the stresses come quickly enough and there is very little emotional support around, will consider suicide and some may try it.

The problems in your lives that pushed you to suicide created a kind of pain that fogged everything and made everything but the pain unimportant. I remember at fifteen suffering severe physical pain from a broken hip. The pain was so bad, so overwhelming, that I would have done anything to get away from it. I wanted morphine (and got it) so I could escape into blackness. The pain of rejection must be like that. Escape is more important than anything else.

But pain doesn't stay constantly at the same level for anyone. When you didn't complete your suicide and life went on, the pain level changed.

Seldom did the source of your problems change. No magic fairy godmother transformed your parents into loving caring people if they were your problem. There was no emotional morphine. Most often the change that made life easier, more possible for you, came from within yourself. That attitude change seemed the strongest, the most permanent change I saw.

The change in your attitude toward yourself was dramatic. You suddenly understood something important about yourself. For some that was that you were alone and you would get no help at home. No one in your family was going to change. Along with this revelation sometimes came the idea that you were valuable in spite of your parents' assessment, that you had been choosing suicide, but it wasn't inevitable. A revelation such as this made a great difference in your attitude and you found that you viewed living quite differently. You found you had more control over life, more opportunities, more future.

More often, the change in your life was not from within. Circumstance changed around you and influenced you. An abusive parent left. You left home. Your parents accepted you. You found a counselor who helped you. Those changes made enough difference in your life that slowly you made other changes for yourself. After a while, you realized that you were coping. Slowly you groped your way out of a fog, step by step, finding a path leading you to a more positive life. You weren't sure you were going to succeed, but, when you looked back down the path at how far you had come, you gained some confidence. Many of you who had tried suicide and not completed it, had achieved a very strong confidence.

Some of you tried to control your feelings by controlling the life around you. You could not control the problems within you so you tried to control everything outside yourself. You found day-to-day living much harder than those who had faced their problems and understood them.

Suzanne understood that she would never obtain the love she wanted from her parents. That knowledge made her strong. Beth did not accept that her parents didn't love her or that her parents' "love" was not helpful to her. Although she told me she was abused as a child, she did not equate that with not being loved.

"I've been living away from home for fifteen months now. I had no self esteem when I first left. But Jim, in the last few months, has been trying to convince me that I'm pretty."

Me: You're absolutely stunning! [She was — auburn curls, green eyes, creamy skin.]

"Oh no. I was raised with, 'You have to lose weight, Beth. You're not pretty. You're not this.'

"If someone said, 'Gee, you look nice,' I'd think 'No, I don't. You're just saying that to make me feel good.' Like I honestly thought I was really, really ugly. So now I'm at the point where I think I don't look half bad. Sure I knew I was intelligent but at the same time they'd [her parents] said I was lazy. And my personality . . . . They said I was bitchy. I cry too much or, 'You're too fat, Beth. Your hair looks like a rat's nest.' or, 'You don't dress right.' I never did anything right. I grew up with it."

Beth was often hit when she was young. Her dad beat her with a belt. At sixteen she hit him back.

"I felt bad. I'd never do it again."

Me: *You* felt bad?

"Well, of course. This is my father. I should respect him."

Me: Do you respect people who hit women?

"My father never laid a hand on my mother."

Me: You're not a woman?

"I think it was because I was his daughter. It's funny we should talk about this because when I was in the ward [psychiatric ward] I heard some awful stories. One girl, her father used to sexually molest her. One, her teacher did and no one believed her. Another, her father used to chase her around with a hatchet."

Me: Did your dad sexually molest you?

"I don't know. I've been told. My mother used to hint at things when I was younger but I don't remember. Nothing when I was a teenager."

So Beth thought that in spite of the treatment she received from her parents, her parents were good and she was bad.

"My parents love me." I heard you say that often. "Love" is a very broad term and I'm not sure any of us knows what we're talking about when we use it. Maybe your parents cared for you in the only way they knew how to care for you. But maybe that kind of "love" wasn't enough. Maybe your parents cared for you, but didn't understand what you needed.

If you felt that they really loved you and cared for you but abused you and neglected you because you were unloveable and basically "bad," then you were co-operating in your own destruction. For some of you that was preferable to admitting that they did not love you. In those circumstances it was very hard to break free of the attitude that you were "no good" and that you were helpless to change your life.

I asked you what you thought had to change before suicide was no longer an option.

Mike and Jake told me that suicide was always an option. Strictly speaking that's true. The possibility of taking your own life is there for you and for everyone. But most of you interpreted the question to mean, when is suicide no longer something you really want to do?

Suzanne said, "I needed to know that somebody was there for me. Maybe, I needed my parents. Like I know that if I went to my mom and said, 'Hey, Mom. I'm considering suicide, will you help me?' She'd say, 'What? Why? It's so stupid.' I'd just kind of slink out of the room. So the rules have to change to, 'Don't put me down. Don't tell me I'm wrong. Just help me.'"

That might never happen in Suzanne's household because she's asking someone else, her mother, to change. And she doesn't have any control over how her mother acts.

Leslie tried to make excuses for her mother. Tried to find a reason why her mother couldn't help her. She did not want to think that her mother did not care.

"I wished she would have talked to me but I always made excuses for her. 'Oh, she's too tired.' 'She's grown up.' 'She's getting old.' 'She has to get up in the morning.' I made all these excuses for why she wouldn't talk to me."

But someone did talk to Leslie. That's what made a huge difference in her life. Two friends spent hours talking to her. They helped her over the very worst of her depression and sustained her through the months to follow. Once Leslie had confidence in herself she was better able to maintain a relationship with her mother.

Sometimes you made a physical change, you left home, because you knew your family patterns were destructive and you could see no way of changing those patterns.

Sometimes you couldn't see that there was anything wrong with your family. You thought all the problems lay within yourself. I met Tanya at a park. We sat on a bench in the sunshine watching the ducks on the water and the children playing on the grass. Tanya was so intelligent that she kept me alert for two hours. She was also so caring and insightful that she taught me a great deal in those two hours.

Tanya saw her parents as loving parents who were trying hard to help her.

"I get constant praise now, after all this [suicide attempts]. And that's pressure in itself. Actually that's the way it's always been. I've always been sort of put upon a pedestal. And they always say to my sister, 'Why can't you be like Tanya? She's so good.' And that's bad for her and it's bad for me. And that means I can never make a mistake. And when I feel myself making mistakes I stop and I pull back and I say to myself, 'What would Dad want?' So that's what I do a lot. The little girl syndrome. Try to please everybody else. If you happen to please yourself by doing that, then that's a bonus.

"My father never tells me what to do. I mean I make my own choices. Whatever I do he always says it's good enough for him. But I feel like it's not.

"I have this vision of my dad as being this god-like perfect kind of man who can impress anyone in the world. Who makes millions of dollars a year, and I can never achieve any of that. And that's where I feel inadequate. Totally inadequate.

"I feel like I hold my family together. See, my parents don't get along very well. As far back as I can remember I've been their mediator. I can remember when I was four or five years old and every time they fought it would be me jumping in the middle saying, 'Please, don't fight. Please, don't fight.' They'd get mad and my dad would grab me by the arm and take me out. He'd leave and I'd go with him. I didn't want to go with him. I wanted to be with my mom. I hated him. He scared me. So I always feel that I have to keep it together. My sister's a basket case. She doesn't know what she wants to do. She just wants to lounge around for the rest of her life. My parents are sort of up in arms about that. I know she feels that I get all the attention. And it's true. I do. I get all the attention which I don't really need.

"Not for a minute do I blame my parents. And I will never blame my parents. If anyone blames my parents, it's themselves. You know, I'm just a victim of circumstance."

Tanya blames herself for her feelings of inadequacy yet she tells me that she had had tremendous pressures put on her to achieve, to be the perfect child, to be the one that held the family together. She doesn't feel valued for what she is, only for what she can do.

When you see the source of your problems as failures in yourself, it is very, very difficult to move past your problems to a happier life. Janet does it with the Alcoholics' Anonymous motto of, "One day at a time."

I was overcome by your courage. I found it hard to do more than two interviews in a day because I had to recover emotionally myself. I left you after a conversation of one and a half to two and a half hours and found a place where I could be alone to just sit. I thought about you and let your emotions sweep over me. I understood the courage it took for you to keep on living and I had to deal with my anger that you should be so alone. You weren't expecting anything from me. You knew that I was collecting information for a book and not a therapist, so you weren't looking for information or help from me. You only wanted to help me write this book.

And while I was sometimes upset at what you had to deal with, I found the hardest thing to bear was the conviction of those who felt they deserved all the troubles they had. I could not deal with that. I was furious with your parents, with your teachers, with myself, with all society that allowed a child to grow up feeling like that. You gave me a hard time. At the same time, those of you who had faced the overwhelming emotional blow of rejection from your parents and had decided to build your life, using your own strengths and your faith in yourself, gave me a tremendous feeling of inspiration. I felt that if you, thirteen, fifteen, seventeen-year-old ordinary people, could do something so difficult, then others could, and there was hope for everyone.

8

ARE YOU A
SUICIDE RISK?

She could have died when she overdosed
Luckily not me
She thought she was pregnant a couple of times
Luckily not me
She was into drugs and booze and sex and fights
Luckily not me

Can she make it before she cracks
and has no place to go
She was on the streets a number of times
No warmth, no food, no clothes

She was deserted more than once
She can't be me, she can't be me.
— Diana

Suicide is not a problem-solver; suicide is an attempt to escape pain. Most of you know that. Suicide does not make life better for you; it ends everything.

Some of you thought you were "crazy," or "weird" to think of suicide. You could talk to your parents about a space station off Mars, organ transplants, extraterrestrial life, but you could not talk about suicide. You were sure that people would think you were crazy. So many of you think that it is wrong, odd or abnormal to think about it. Well, many teens do think about it.

How dangerous is it to think about suicide? Not dangerous at all to think about it. How close are teens getting to actually trying suicide when they think about it? Everyone should try to assess that for themselves. So many of you experienced the same feelings, tried to cope in the same way, that your behaviors can be warning signs to others that help is needed. None of the symptoms of stress I'm going to talk about are indicators of suicide by themselves, but the symptoms compound; that is, one symptom plus another symptom equals many times the stress. So the more signs a person has, the closer he is to attempting suicide — theoretically. But that doesn't take into consideration how very different everyone is. There are some people who exhibit many of the following signs of stress and never consider suicide. My son told me, "Don't get fixed on suicide. Some kids have the same problems and have other ways of coping." Not everyone with these symptoms tries suicide; but many do. Most of you who tried suicide had a cluster of symptoms that included the things I'm going to talk about now.

Try to think of these suicide stress symptoms in the way you'd think of cold symptoms. A person who has a cold is not abnormal. They just have a cold. Their body is overwhelmed by the cold virus and can't cope with it so they show the symptoms of a cold. A person invaded by problems can be overwhelmed by thoughts of suicide. Instead of the sore throat and runny nose that tells you she has a cold, this person shows suicide stress symptoms. They are indicators of a problem.

The first area where many of you had problems was your family. You may have loved your parents, but felt that one or both of them wished you would leave home, wished you would change, wished you would be a different person, or wished you would stay away from them. One or both of your parents may not have accepted you. Sometimes they accepted you conditionally; that is, they accepted you as long as you got good grades, dressed well, met their standards. You knew that no matter how hard you tried to please them, they would never be happy because they didn't really love every part of you, and all their criticism was just a way of telling you that.

You may have responded to this rejection by withdrawing from them, by spending a lot of time in your room or spending a lot of time away from home. This isolation spread until you spent very little time with any person, including the people who used to be your friends. You didn't yell, scream, argue or demand attention. You just quietly withdrew from family and friends until you lived a lonely life, not interacting with anyone.

If you lived out of town, you found it easier to be isolated. It seemed hard to find a network of friends in the country where teens lived several miles from each other. Teenage years can contain short periods of intense loneliness. That brief feeling can be intensified where young people may have both the feelings of loneliness and the reality of no one else around.

This intense loneliness can occur also in the city. You can feel lonely in the middle of the school cafeteria. When you were engulfed in this loneliness you often did not reach out to anyone. You learned a way of dealing with your rejection. You withdrew. It may not have been a way that solved the problem but it relieved your feelings and allowed you to function right then.

You may have responded to rejection from your parents by talking only about what they wanted to talk about. You seldom brought up your own ideas. They responded to your withdrawal and isolation by "putting you down," ridiculing you, name-calling, telling you you were stupid, lazy, worthless and no-good. Of course, not all parents did this but some parents seemed to spend a lot of time yelling at you. This made you feel even more unloved. Some parents physically abused you, hit you with fists or weapons, although this usually happened less often as you got older. Some parents had an on-going attitude of rejection that resulted in continual put-downs, such as locking you out of the house, turning off porch lights when you were out to remind you you were not welcome home, omitting to set a place for you at the table, arranging family outings to exclude you, talking about you to others when you were present as if you were invisible. You felt powerless. You usually saw no way of changing the pattern.

Sometimes the put-downs were more subtle. You might have been told what your faults were and then been told that your mother, father, brother was only "teasing." You felt attacked and then confused because the attacker said you were over-reacting, that he was only "teasing". Teasing is a form of aggression. Your initial reaction was usually correct. You were being attacked.

Sometimes parents committed small, insidious, repeated acts that resulted in your feeling incompetent. Perhaps your mother made your bed and straightened your room every day. Wouldn't that be a "nice" thing to do? Somehow you felt that your privacy was invaded, that your mother was telling you that you were still a little girl, that you needed looking after, that you were not competent.

These subtle behaviors made you feel uncomfortable. You knew there was something wrong, but you couldn't define it. Nothing your family did seemed "serious" enough to warrant such an emotional reaction on your part.

Very often, your feelings were correct. Subtle, small and constant pressures can cause big problems in self-concept. For instance, if you asked a parent a question and he or she simply didn't answer, that made you feel unimportant, almost invisible. It helps to know that *most* people would feel degraded in that situation. Your feelings are valid.

Many teenagers automatically tense when a parent says either, "Because I love you, I want to tell you . . . " or "For your own good . . . " Those remarks are usually a cover for criticism. It is quite okay to feel hurt. It is quite okay for teens to trust their own reactions.

In many families no one talked to you about sex. No one talked to you about anything important, but particularly about sex. No one told you the practical, real facts of life. No one told you about sexual feelings, how you should act in this situation, in that situation. Even now, in the supposedly frank times of today, some of you found yourselves handicapped by not enough sexual knowledge. You felt as though everyone but you knew the rules.

Some of you didn't know how to handle the sexual pressures that you got at school from your friends. You got involved with the sexual practices of your group before you really made a decision about it. No one helped you find out whether that behavior would make you happy. Many of you were accused of sexual promiscuity, sleeping around, when you were innocent. "Slut" and "whore" came at you from your parents, usually without justification, and made you feel hurt and bewildered. Sometimes, your parents (or parent) were unsure of their own sexuality and some were conducting affairs and had casual sexual alliances themselves. When you hit puberty your parents (parent) projected their worst fears onto you and made these accusations. They didn't help you and they didn't stop their accusations no matter how innocent you were. Most of you in these conditions gave up trying to prove your innocence and went looking for sexual experience.

Movies and television make sex seem a sport. Yet you learned fast that sexual acts carry emotions with them and can be confusing, painful and even humiliating.

It's not abnormal to be confused about sex especially when you are first learning about it. It always amazes me that we expect teens to know all about sex, somehow. We give math instructions so they can learn to add but we rarely give much information on such an important subject as sex. Some of you have had no information and little encouragement to become aware of your sexuality. In spite of the books that tell us we should all be more open and honest about sex, teens are still told to ignore their sexuality, pretend their bodies haven't changed, their feelings haven't matured, pretend they are still little girls and boys and ignore this exciting, interesting, lovable, new person. And somehow, magically, everyone will understand sex.

The conflict this created in you very often added to your stress, but seemed to add to your inclination to suicide only when you couldn't talk about it with your parents.

Many of you responded to your increasingly difficult life by getting lower grades at school. You started skipping classes. (Why go when you'll just get hassled for not doing your work?) Or, you got good grades but they were still not good enough for your parents.

When you felt that you were worthless and nothing was going right, everything overwhelmed you. You may have dressed to reflect that. You might have ignored what you wore and put clothes on only to escape arrest for indecency, or you might have paid a great deal of attention to your clothes and tried to create a costume to hide in. You might have dressed all in black and made your face dead-white, or have worn long hair that hid your eyes. You may have been trying on costumes to see how they made you feel, or you may have been using your clothes as a screen from the world.

When you felt you couldn't cope you spent a lot of time daydreaming. Daydreaming can be a harmless escape for all of us (it keeps me sane in bank and grocery line-ups) but it can be a day-long fantasy world that takes people away from real life. Many of you remembered that just before you tried suicide you spent long hours daydreaming. Along with this went your inability to concentrate. You just couldn't seem to bring your mind to pay attention to anything. You felt as if you were always half asleep. Sometimes you had an out-of-body experience as if you were sitting back and looking at yourself going through the day.

You sometimes changed your eating habits. You ate much more, stuffing yourself in the hope you would gain weight and become ugly, or starving yourself in the hope you'd disappear. You sometimes changed your sleeping patterns. Many had trouble going to sleep at night and woke very early in the morning.

When you were feeling rejected and depressed you were prone to accidents. This might have been your way of flirting with death. You started physical fights and had sudden bursts of violence — some of you, some of the time. Sometimes you attacked yourself, carved your arms with a knife, cut off the circulation to parts of your body. Sometimes, your rejection of yourself was less obvious. You were very uncomfortable with compliments, for instance, and thought a person who compliments you was lying. You did things that invited criticism, didn't do your homework, and then felt that the resulting criticism was because you were unloveable.

One of the problems of people who have been rejected by their parents and who have low self-esteem is their fixed idea that they don't deserve happiness. If they do feel happy they are sure that it won't last, that they will have to pay for moments of happiness with corresponding moments of unhappiness. Often they can't accept happiness and make sure they do something to send it away.

Sometimes a movie or television show can influence a teen's decision to kill herself. She might watch a movie that makes a young girl's death by OD'ing seem like a peaceful, beautiful way to escape life. The movie didn't show the spasms and contortions a body goes through when affected by drugs, or the inevitable mess from vomiting. Movies aren't real, the viewer knows that, but they *seem* real and a teen may feel in sympathy with the character who died. Be aware that you may be susceptible to the influence of movies and television when you are depressed and suicidal. You should be aware that a romantic drama about the "peace" of suicide is going to be dangerously seductive and perhaps you should not watch it. You should seek out a documentary or a factual discussion of suicide, so you can get information. You need help in the real world, you don't need a fantasy.

Many of you had tried suicide more than once. As Suzanne said, "Once you try it, it's easier to do it the second time." Sometimes you tried actions that didn't kill you right then but would at some time, like habitual drinking. Or you tried actions that might kill you and might not, risky things, like reckless driving, or mixing drugs, or mixing drugs and alcohol, running through traffic, walking on the outside ledges of buildings. Look at some of the things you do and wonder if you are trying hold death close with one hand while gripping hard to life with the other.

It may be that those who are thinking of suicide may have had a death in the family when they were young. Some one you cared about died and that made death seem comfortable. You may feel that you will go to that loved one in death. You have no assurance that this is so but, because you want care and comfort so badly, you *believe* that the loved person will be waiting. You think you will have the "happily ever after" ending of the fairy story.

Some teens may have had a death in their family when they were young and been impressed with the way their parents reacted to that death. Maybe their parents showed no emotion at all except relief. Maybe they cried and protested love when it was too late. As young children, some teens saw such reactions and remembered them. They may have imagined that their parents would react to their death in the same way. Rarely did these teens have a chance to talk to anyone about how they felt at the time. If someone in your family or a friend died by suicide you will be more likely to think suicide is appropriate for you.

Even if you had someone you could talk to, it wasn't always possible to describe what you felt. You often didn't know if you were bored, angry, hurt, confused, depressed. You felt foolish telling anyone anything. All you knew was your feelings were over-whelming. If you weren't used to expressing your feelings, you didn't find it easy and you might have found you had to meet with a friend or counselor two or three times before you started to talk about what was *really* bothering you.

If your usual method of dealing with problems was to get an-gry and say nothing and blame yourself then you may have seen suicide as only what you deserved. You thought a jerk-head like you could die and never be missed. You were used to blaming yourself and to looking no farther than your own personality for the source of the problems. You thought that you weren't good enough to live. Your attitude that you didn't matter and that you were worthless wasn't a real assessment. After all, people who don't even know you don't want you to die. (I don't. The publisher doesn't. The crisis center people don't. Thousands of people don't want you to die.) Many people value you intrinsically. Value you as you are. You may *feel* worthless but that doesn't mean that you are worthless.

When parents, teachers, other teens put you down many of you felt that you deserved it, that those smarter, more together, people knew the *real* you. Since they knew the *real* you and thought you were worthless, then you must be worthless. You believed their evaluation of you. It was as though you held up a mirror to them so that you could see yourself and they reflected an ugly image back to you. You believed their transformation of you, their image of you. You lost track of the *real* you.

Your self-esteem was so low that everyday problems became proof that you were no good. You could not put yourself up against one thousand teens your age and tell yourself that you were really alright. You didn't feel alright. You felt second class. If anyone told you how good you were, you thought they had poor taste and lousy judgement.

Self-esteem, feeling good about yourself, feeling valuable isn't a black and white characteristic. It isn't something people either have or don't have. Self-esteem is a characteristic everyone has to some extent. Some people have a great deal of it, and some people have very little. It's common to say a person has "no" self-esteem. "Low" self-esteem is probably a more accurate term because self-esteem is a matter of degree. Some people have more than others. Everyone has more or less self-esteem at different times in their lives. If they have very low self-esteem now that doesn't mean they will have very low self-esteem forever. It means that if they realize that they have very low self-esteem now they should treat that as a serious problem and try to find how they can increase it. People who have low self-esteem expect very little happiness. People who have a lot of self-esteem expect a lot of happiness. It seems that these expectations are to some extent self-fulfilling prophecies. People often set out to *make* happen what they *expect* to happen.

Many of you thought of death as an escape where you would be safe. You thought you would *feel* better when you were dead. You thought of death as a temporary state where you could hide in safety for a time. Sometimes you thought you would be watching the activities of your family and friends. Sometimes you thought you would be able to comment on what they were doing and how they were feeling.

For some of you a moment came when you understood that death is final. Suddenly you understood that you would not come back. You would not have a fairy tale ending. You would not be part of the life you left behind. For some of you that shook you into taking sober responsibility for your own happiness. Often, that didn't occur until the pressures and pain slackened and you had a refuge—a friend's house, an aunt's place, the hospital, some safe environment where you could recover and begin to feel better about yourself.

For some of you a moment came when you realized that no matter how many times you tried suicide, you did not control your parents' ability to care about you. You faced that fact. For you, that was the time you started building a life of your own. That was very hard to do and often only possible when you had a strong love for another, or a strong network of friends. But some of you managed this with very little support. You have my admiration.

The emotions that went with your suicidal actions were many and varied but they seem to stem from your feelings of rejection and low self-esteem. When these feelings got more than you could bear, you began to plan to kill yourself. You felt fogged with pain and didn't see any future so you stopped making plans for the future and you may have done some or all of these "Red Flag" actions.

1. You gave away prized possession, your stereo, your television, even small sentimental articles.

2. You made final arrangements, wrote a note, gave instructions to your friends.

3. You started telling people, "I can't go on," or "All I want to do is die." The problem with these statements as indicators of suicidal intention was that many of your teen friends did not react to them. They thought it was just extravagant language like, "He blew me away," or "I thought I'd die." They didn't pick up on the despair.

When people are in this vulnerable state they may feel that they have no one, absolutely no one, to talk to.

A combination of losses can result in overwhelming despair. A loss can be a move to a different neighborhood with the resulting loss of old friends. It can be Dad or Mom moving out of the house. It can be the death of a grandparent. It can even be the death of a pet. Loss can be a girl friend or boyfriend moving away or just losing interest. The loss is important to the individual; it may not seem important to anyone else. Any loss can be enough to trigger suicide.

This isn't a complete list. These are just some of the ways people indicate they are thinking of suicide. We all need to be alert for these signs in our classrooms, at work, in our families.

9

HOW YOU CAN HELP YOURSELF

She's got to make good
*   got to make good*
No one wants to listen to the little girl cry
The little girl pretends too well
*   too well*
The little girl can run fast
*   can run faster than anyone*
She chooses to sit in a wheelchair and cry
*   and cry*
She's the only one who can help herself
*   who can help*
Everyone's too busy
Everyone.
— T.S.

When you were in pain, when suicide appeared as an escape, you often did not have the energy or the ability to make big changes in your life. You often were not able to see clearly what you needed. If a white knight had come out of the sky and invited you to ride away, you would have escaped with him in a flash. But white knights were in short supply and you usually had to deal with your problems yourself. Nothing in your real world looked worthwhile.

When you were in pain, every path looked too hard to take, every option too difficult to try. If you had advice at that time it should have been, don't try to make grand changes. Try to make small ones, perhaps just one small change.

Some of you couldn't talk to your parents. You'd tried that and you felt helpless about *ever* being able to break through to them. You recognized that you needed acceptance from your parents and love and understanding that you saw others had. You recognized that you wanted that and yet saw no way of getting it. Most of you didn't talk to your sisters or brothers. Suzanne sometimes talked to her brother and Mike to his sister. Some people did have a favorite relative. You usually couldn't talk to your teachers. Anna talked to her teacher but only briefly and not intimately. There doesn't seem to be enough time in your school schedules to develop the kind of relationship with a teacher that would make it possible to confide in him or her.

Suicide seemed to be a taboo subject, one of those social unmentionables that was not discussed very often. Some of you felt even talking about suicide was "wrong," a shameful idea, and you didn't want to admit to even thinking about it. You thought that anyone you talked to would either tell you you were crazy or tell you you were wrong to think about it. That's true. Some people would tell you "not to be dumb." Usually, the only person you felt safe talking to was a friend.

It was often best to talk to a friend who had tried suicide and no longer wanted that escape. Two of you told me that you had talked to people who were also suicidal and that they had no energy to help you. You needed to talk to someone who was sensible and "together," and who would take you seriously.

It is sometimes very hard to reach someone who can help. If you are looking for a listener it might help to make a list of everyone you know who can help and then start at the top of the list and ask each one until you find someone. It's harder to deal with rejection from someone if you have no idea whom to approach next. It's easier if you have a list of "possibles."

Some people won't listen. They feel uncomfortable talking about suicide and they don't want to hear about it. They can't stand intimacy. They aren't used to intimacy. They feel incompetent themselves and threatened by other people's revelations and they won't listen when a teen approaches for help.

It is often necessary to try several friends. If they won't listen you must be prepared to feel rejected, foolish and even more worthless than before. Most people would feel that way. Be prepared to hit a few duds. Finding a listening friend is the most important thing in your life right now and you need to keep trying.

It is important for you to see yourself in a long-term relationship with your family. Everything doesn't have to be changed today. There is probably no quick-fix solution, no fifty-minute problem solver like a television drama, no sudden revelation illuminating your parents' minds to what a great person you really are. Change in the relationship with your parents takes time, perhaps years. Most adults are still working on improving their relationship with their own parents. It helps to set goals with your parents, or rather goals that concern your parents, two-week goals, two-month goals, two-year goals. Then get help.

Some of you had little practice at dealing with stress, even small stresses. You learned ways of coping but it would have been helpful if you had known some simple exercises that you could have used. Try to understand what your body needs and work on some technique of body control that helps you. These are often taught in aerobics classes, gym class at school or meditation groups. These exercises may help some but they don't do much to relieve the overwhelming pain of a suicidal person. They may help the day to day little problems that add to stress. But frankly, they don't help as much as a good friend who listens. Some of you changed your environment. You quit school, moved to another city, moved out of your house, went to live with a sister, a boyfriend, a boyfriend's parents, moved into an apartment of your own, moved onto the streets. Diana was fifteen years old. She met me for coffee towing her boyfriend behind. He had tried suicide also so stayed to be interviewed. Diana had been abandoned by her mother at five and her grandmother at ten. At fourteen she moved into a park. Truly, she lived there for several months, using her boyfriend's mother's house as a place to wash and change.

Sometimes this change in your life relieved you of the constant criticism, the pressure of the put-downs from your parents. The easing of the pressure was enough to allow you to gather your personality together and let you gain strength. If you moved out to an atmosphere where you were accepted (you didn't need to to be loved, just accepted) then you seemed to be able to re-assess yourself, and start to like yourself.

There seemed to be few places you could go. Most of you told me that you had no place to go. You thought that the world outside your home was unsafe. You watched TV and you read the "Do not hitch-hike" signs, and you paid attention to warnings that the world was rough. You watched a movie about street kids and drugs and prostitution. The world outside your house, outside your social circle, looked dangerous. That worried me quite a lot. Why didn't the world outside your family look like an adventure? You told me it looked dangerous. Your low self-esteem might be responsible for this attitude that while others could "make it" out there in the world, you could not.

There also seems to be a "cult of excellence" weighing down on you. Parents, teachers, ads on television, newspaper stories, tell you that you must succeed, you must be the very best! Not the very best you can be, but you must be better than everyone else. That didn't seem to be a problem when I was a teenager. I knew perfectly well I wasn't the best in anything. Why can't you have a more reasonable life plan? Why couldn't you plan to take your time, be happy, grow easily? Why this frantic rush? It seemed that everyone was afraid that you'd fail. You were afraid you'd fail. You were already suffering from a loss of self-esteem and you didn't think you deserved a job. It all looked overwhelming.

So what can you do if you can't make the major change of leaving home? Find a friend to talk to. Try calling the crisis center, the distress center, the helpline (telephone numbers are on the inside front cover of the phone book). There may be some phone books that do not list this, but the number can be found from the telephone information service. If you live out of a city and are in trouble, you can call the operator and ask for help. The operators will put you through to the nearest distress center and will stay on the line until someone answers. If you talk to someone at a distress center and don't think they are helping, you can try again at another time and talk to someone else. The idea is to keep trying.

You can search out a community resource by checking the bulletin board at school for information or checking the telephone book. Community agencies are listed in the front of the phone book or under "Family Services" in the white pages. You can phone the Family Services office and ask where you can get counseling help.

The usual, normal, common way to find help is to get a phone number, phone that number, then get a referral phone number from there and phone that number, then get another referral number from there and phone it. It's a tedious process. You will have to tell each person who answers the same story. But stay with it. It is common to go this three-phone-call route before you actually get to the person you want to talk to—not at a distress center. They answer directly there. But at the family services' centers or other mental health centers, where a receptionist answers the phone, it is better to say, "Can you tell me where I can get a counselor for suicide prevention?" rather than, "I'm thinking of suicide." Receptionists want to hear questions they can answer. One day in October, I called the Family Service Center near me. I got an answering service. Someone phoned me back four hours later. I called the Mental Health Clinic, the phone rang twelve times before a receptionist answered. If you call a helping center, you may have to persist: keep calling, until you get help. The person you finally reach can usually help.

Sometimes, when you most need help, you don't have the energy it takes to ask for it. You feel "depressed," so tired all the time that you can't pick up the phone and dial. Even in those situations you can usually ask a friend to help you. Your friend can stay with you while you talk to the worker on the phone.

Sometimes, you feel restless, as if you couldn't settle down to anything, even phoning a counselor. You spin in a world of activity faster and faster because, if you stopped, you'd have to feel, and you don't want to feel anything. Ask a friend to help you.

Some schools have peer counselors. These may be students

who have tried suicide and moved past those feelings in their lives or who are gifted with great compassion and who can understand what other teens are feeling. They are available, usually, through the counselor or, in a small school, by asking friends.

Talking to someone immediately is very important. Everyone has a need to be understood and accepted. In time, some things may change. In time, the affairs that were pressuring your parents might pass and they might turn to you and help. Rena's parents were shocked at her suicide attempt. They had not known she was so depressed and disturbed. They immediately began talking to her, helping her, trying to understand her. However, only two persons I talked to received attention from their parents. But other aspects of your life might change if you talk to an understanding listener and keep hope alive.

You can develop a support system, as Teresa did, of friends, parents of friends and work-mates. This support system reflects a positive image of you and makes you feel more worthwhile. Feeling worthwhile is important to everyone. It is important to maintain your self-esteem while the world around you makes slow changes. And you will find that an increase in your self-esteem brings on a decrease in your need for suicide.

10

WHAT OTHER PEOPLE CAN DO FOR YOU

When i turn out the Light
and go to bed
i lie hoping for a new and better tomorrow
But thoughts of reality creep from the shadows
in which I try to keep them hidden
during the Brightness of my days.
They tell me there are no promises, no guarantees
and no assurances. There is emptiness, loneliness,
fear, guilt, shame
And I allow no tears, though they do want me
Tomorrow is new but
will it bring peace and laughter and acceptance.
i will get lost in tomorrow,
like today, like yesterday.
i will cry where no one can see—inside.
and drown a little more beneath those tears. i will
hold them tightly and safely, and will not let them go
like i wish someone would do to me.
— Tanya
(adapted from a longer poem)

Other people can give you emotional support and caring attention. It's okay to be needy, to be in need of support and attention.

It is possible to get this kind of caring from a friend. Teens need strong friendships. They need to feel accepted by friends. Such a friend may help them to make small, important changes in their family lives. Families are like spider webs with interlocking threads of relationships. Move one thread and all the threads move. Make one change in a relationship and all the relationships adjust and change. It is often difficult to talk to anyone in your family but you can try other ways of reaching them besides direct conversation. You can record a message on a tape deck and leave it for your parents to hear when you are not there. You can leave a letter to be read by your parents. You can ask a school counselor to come home to talk with you to your parents. You can ask a crisis worker to come home to help you. You can ask a minister, or social worker to meet at your house with your parents. You may be helped by this. On the other hand, you may not cause any changes at all in your family. You may be more discouraged, but you may have earned a friend in the social worker or the minister.

You can try role playing your problems with a friend. Ask the friend or two or three friends to take the place of your parents and try talking to them as if they were your parents. Friends listening to you role play can give suggestions. This might give you confidence when you approach your parents. Most of you don't have a group of friends who would give serious thought to your problem. Many of you have one friend, though, who would listen. You must start with the idea that you are valuable, you are worth helping and then spend time helping yourself.

Look into your community for help. It is organized so that counselors, psychiatrists, ministers, hospital staff and crisis workers are supposed to help you. You told me that often, they do not. There are no guarantees that if you ask for help you will get it from the first person you contact. You have to keep looking. Professionals should help you. They should be competent, well-trained, experienced and caring. But they have the disadvantage of being human, of sometimes not being "good enough" for you. You may have to work with less than perfect counselors to try to help yourself.

Leslie could not go down the stairs to the apartment below and talk to her mother or father. She had no friends she could confide in so she went to her school counselor who was more interested in getting Leslie's school number, feeding it into the computer and looking at the computer picture of Leslie (her grades, her school absences, her tardiness) than in looking across the desk at the suicidal girl who was crying for help. There are people like that, but not all are like that.

When Janet could not talk to her grandparents she tried the school counselor. However, her school counselor did not have much ability to counsel. "I spent a lot of time in her office, from the second semester until June, and I didn't get anywhere with her. She was a really nice person but . . . it was really boring. I told her I was a schizophrenic [Janet was not] and she couldn't figure me out. And, like, the counselor said everything was confidential but the word got around. So the counselor told one teacher and she told another one and pretty soon everyone was coming up to me and saying, 'Oh you poor child.' Right? 'Go to hell,' was my answer. I got really mad at her. It shows they care but I didn't need her talking about me." Janet felt cheated of a helper, understandably, since the counselor was not keeping her confidence.

Everyone who goes to school should be able to reach a professional through the school counselor or the local mental health association. But some of you live in small towns, or go to schools where there is only one counselor whom everyone knows is not good. Some of you live where you have more choice and you still find it hard to get help the first time you try. Even at the time of your suicide attempt when your need for help was the greatest, you met put-downs and put-offs by the people you expected to help you, the hospital staff. You expected the hospital staff, the nurses and doctors, to be understanding but many of you met hostility and anger.

While Tanya and I absorbed the sunshine of the park and the peace and tranquility around us she told me about her second suicide attempt. She got the same nurse at the hospital as she had had the first time. "The nurse sat down with me and said, 'What the hell's your problem? This is the second time in two months. Do you really think we have the time for you? We need our time for really sick people.' I thought she'd just given me another reason for dying. I said, 'I'm sorry. I'm sorry. I'm sorry for existing.' That's how I felt."

Bruce was in the hospital at thirteen with a suicide attempt. The doctors kept him him four hours, pumped his stomach, asked him why he did it. He didn't know. He went home without any follow-up or recommendations for counseling.

Robert was taken to the hospital by a cab driver who could see he was very sick. The hospital phoned his parents. His parents sent him to the family doctor who said, "This is stupid. Do you realize that you would have been hurting your family if you had killed yourself?" Robert thought it would have been much better if the doctor had asked him, "Why did you do it in the first place?" A lecture, is not counseling.

Now for the good news. Some people did help you a great deal. Beth got help from her family doctor. "She set us [Beth and her family] up with a psychiatrist and we went and saw her. Well, just me. They [her parents] went once but that was farther along." When Beth tried suicide again her mother called the family doctor who called the psychiatrist. The psychiatrist told her mother to take Beth to the hospital right away. The family doctor suggested the adolescent ward at Vancouver General Hospital.

"So I went there and they talked to me for six hours and tested me and everything and they asked, 'Do you want to enter, to admit yourself? You don't have to.' I said, 'Yes, I do.' I was really scared. I'd drunk a whole bottle of vodka. I threw up a lot.

"They stuck a tube down my throat. I remember that. My mother was seeing an analyst so she had a whole bunch of drugs. Lithium. She used to be on Tranxene and Lithium. I know she has to take one pill to wake herself up in the morning and another to go to bed.

"I went in. At first I was going into the psychiatric assessment unit. And I don't know, I didn't think I was one of them. But anyway I stayed there about a week and then they transferred me to East 2, a teenage unit. There were rooms for two girls or one girl. There were ten there. They were all teenagers and everything was done on a point and merit system. In the daytime we had things where we'd work together and talk. We all ate meals together. There was a TV room. We did our own laundry. Every night we had a hour of quiet time and there were psych. nurses that would come around and talk to you. They were always there. You saw a doctor every two days or so.

"It was really good. If you ever felt you were going to blow it, they had a room with pads on the floor, with pads and pillows and a blanket and it was for you. There was like a merit system. We were all at Stage 3. There were other stages where you had to stay in your room, and eat in your room. You'd get all your privileges taken away from you. As you went up you got to go out. On Stage 1 you could go out in the hospital grounds and on another you could go out of the hospital grounds if they knew exactly where you were going. You could have a day pass or a weekend pass if your doctor felt it was okay.

"The doctor was good. He said, 'It's not Beth's problem. It's the whole family's problem.' So he got the whole family and myself in and gave us communication help. And I can still go and see him on an outpatient basis. It went along fine for almost a year and then I left home."

Not many of you got that kind of support and help but there is help like that out there.

Megan had had what she thought was a pretty good relationship with her social worker. She told the social worker about her attempted suicide by overdosing. "I didn't want to tell my mom at the time. And I haven't told her yet. The social worker was all for telling my mom and marching me to the emergency hospital. I didn't want that. I stopped talking to her [the social worker]. I found talking to my friend helped a lot more. The social worker couldn't handle it. And by this time I was trying to talk to my mom more."

Bruce found some help from a corrections office and from some agencies. "The John Howard Society was good. That helped. The Salvation Army was good too, especially during my time at WYO [Juvenile Detention Home]. They are like the commercial says. They're there to lend a hand. They overlook your problems and make you feel at home."

There are no guarantees that you will get help when you ask for it. Sometimes you hesitated to ask for help because you didn't know how the person you were going to approach would feel. How do people feel when you ask them for help? Sometimes they open up and love you. They have generous souls. They may have been in despair at some point in their lives and they understand you. They are glad you asked them for help because you make them feel useful and worthy. They may even be grateful that you talked to them. Many people feel this way.

Some people feel uncomfortable. They feel incompetent dealing with problems. So they try to pretend that your problems are not serious, and that you don't truly *need* help. This makes it easier for them not to respond to you. Understand that. They can't. Try someone else. Don't waste energy blaming the ones that can't help. You are asking for something they can't give. Find someone who can. There is a network for you, a group of people who want to know and care about you.

11

ADVICE FROM
OTHER TEENS

I see my reflection
As I sit poolside
Yet the rippled mirror
Shows no more than my features
   Anyone could look at me now
And not know what I've been through.
—Rena

Many of you had lived through years of painful experiences. You had tried suicide more than once and had lived with the humiliation, rejection and emotional trauma that had come with your suicide attempts. What did you think other teens might do? When you looked back on your lives what do you think you should have done? You had lived with families who made life hard. You had lived with attitudes in yourselves that made life hard. You had come to believe in your families' negative images. And you had come through all that. How did your manage? What did help?

You told me that you had to make some changes. Sometimes the changes were very small, but a change allowed you to move on. Several of you made changes in your personal lives. Leslie said, "I've come to the point where it's me that matters." She had thought that she had to preserve her family. She had to be the one who kept everything together. She felt free and strong when she decided that she was important, and that *she* mattered. Leslie didn't just decide this one fine day. After her suicide attempt she had to go through a very hard process of talking things out and trying to understand herself. But it was this attitude, *I'm important*, that made a difference to her.

Amy learned a changed attitude slowly over time. She tried suicide many times and finally, when she was about eighteen, she realized that she had been growing past a lot of her problems. "I had to give life another chance. There was always something. I knew it would always get better. Things always do. I can talk to my friends now. Suicide didn't do anything." This attitude change took time and experience. She had to live past the worst of her problems before she believed enough in herself to think she could handle life. No one came by and rescued her. She looked at her life, talked out her problems and rescued herself.

Teresa found her own strength after several years of trying suicide. "After the Anacin bit [a suicide attempt], it was just like I had to take my life in my own hands because no one else was going to help. It was like a one-woman crusade type of thing. I was going to be the best I could be and nobody was going to stop me. I don't let people stop me now."

Rena wrote me a letter three months after our interview. She said, "Tell them there *are* people who care. But they can't help alone. You yourself have to let them help.

"The main thing is to feel good about yourself. You're not conceited if you love and respect yourself. Only healthy."

Leslie and Amy and Teresa didn't find strength within themselves right away. They found help from outside themselves first. When people tell you that you should "just buckle down and take charge of yourself" they didn't understand that you couldn't. Not at that moment. Leslie and Amy and Teresa had to live through many failures before they found help, strength, direction and a feeling that they were okay. Once they had that feeling of being worthwhile, important, admirable even, then they could handle life.

Many of you advised other teens, who were living such a difficult life that suicide looked reasonable, to find someone who can help.

Robert said, "Find somebody to talk to. Listen to what he has to say. Don't hang around your parents if they are the cause of your problems. They try to hold on and that's just going to make you worse. My parents don't want me to make mistakes but I learn better if I do make mistakes. If need be, even run away for a while. Stay with a friend. Find a friend who you can talk to, who will listen to what you have to say. I think if I was faced with it again, I'd probably run away this time. That seems to be the other way, rather than suicide, a smarter way."

Robert did talk to workers at the crisis center quite a few times. He found them always ready to listen when he needed someone to listen. "The crisis center was so good that they said, 'If things are so bad at home, we can find you a place to stay.' And that was just great. That's what I needed to hear. As long as I had someone to talk to, it was okay. If I didn't have them to talk to I don't know what would have happened. I wouldn't be here right now.

"I called them every week. They wanted me to call and tell them what I'd been going through. There wasn't anyone else. I couldn't talk to my parents. I couldn't talk to my friends because they all thought I was . . . weird. The crisis center were the ones that asked me how I was feeling, what I wanted to do. That's what I liked above anything. Asking me. It was the first time I'd felt important. After my ordeal at the hospital I phoned them up. They didn't say, 'You stupid. Why did you do this?' It was like, 'You must have really needed someone to talk to.' It was so fantastic that someone would understand like that."

Tanya felt the importance of having someone to talk to. "You have to take the first step and say, 'Hey. I need help!' And if the first person doesn't help you, you have to find somebody else." Tanya told me how hard it was to reach out to someone else. "You don't want to admit there's something wrong with you. You know down inside that there is, but you don't want to admit it. You're ashamed. You're really ashamed. You can't handle it." You also didn't realize that there are many teens who felt the way you did and you thought that you were the only one. If not the only one in the world, at least the only one in your school or your neighborhood or your gang. "My parents, my dad, is really successful in what he does, well-respected. For me to go to him and say, 'Dad, I can't handle life . . . .' I couldn't do it. I had to have somebody go and do it for me."

So many of you thought that you had to handle all your problems by yourself. You didn't want to be dependent on other kids, or helping professionals. You wanted to do it yourself. You didn't think of accepting help in dealing with your emotional life. Or, you didn't know how to get help with your emotional life.

Suzanne, fifteen, asked me to pass on her advice. She said to tell other teens, "Think about it. Remember that there is someone out there, always, even if you have to go looking for them. That's what you really need. Someone to tell you that you're okay."

One of the more interesting self-help groups I came across was Megan's group of friends. Megan had three friends who were loyal and committed to a deep friendship. They went to the same school and listened to each other's problems. They were alert for signs of depression.

"If one of the girls is depressed we'll spend the night with her. Or two of us or all three of us. We never stay at one person's house over and over, like it always changes. Usually if one girl is depressed, the others will treat her to supper. Like we'll all chip in and pay for her. One of the girls doesn't like having us pay for her and we know that she doesn't like it so we let her pay. It's got to the point where we know what everybody likes in food too and we try to get the depressed person's favorite food. If I'm really depressed they pick me up after school. We drop all our books at Tara's house and Tara and me and the other two will go out. It's all okay with our folks. We usually go for pizza. And we'll sit down and order a huge pizza, ham and pineapple, huge pops and we'll sit there. We'll get there at five o'clock and we'll sit there like until it closes at one [a.m.] and we'll talk.

"It all started just at the beginning of this year and it really, really helps a lot.

"Talking about suicide has helped me see that it's final. If someone's depressed we'll talk about it and try to figure out *why* they're depressed and suicidal."

Me: How do you figure out why?

"We ask. They tell us. Like I've got this problem and I know they'll say, 'You're not alone.' Sometimes when someone's really depressed and I ask them why they're depressed and they say, 'Oh, because I got a bad grade on my test,' and we can tell like that's not the truth so we'll go have pizza or we'll go have hamburgers and we'll figure out why."

Me: Do you ever get into things you can't handle?

"I think if I were by myself, like just one on one, I might do that. But, because there are three of us listening, we just keep talking until we help."

Since most of you told me that you wouldn't talk to adults, or you didn't know any adults you could talk to, Megan's mutual caring group seems to be a great way to deal with problems. If you have tried suicide yourself you are better able to understand someone else's preoccupation with it. You can see the problems that others ignore and you can help because you, after all, have had the problems and managed to still stay living.

Many of you told me that you felt you had to help others at school, even teens you barely knew, when you saw that they were depressed or when you realized that they were thinking about suicide. You were unlikely to pretend that their worries weren't serious, and you didn't ridicule them, or put them down with sarcasm or a joke. You understood and you did help. You were a very powerful friend. Sometimes another teen is all the help a suicidal teen has. Since suicide is the second most frequent cause of death in teenagers, and teenagers see other teens as their first lifeline, they are very important to each other.

Some teens run into the problem of the "deadly secret." A friend confides his suicidal plans to you and asks that you tell no one. You are worried that your friend will try suicide yet, at the same time, you're worried that if you "tell" his parents or a teacher, your friend will deny it, tell everyone that you betrayed him and make you feel like a louse or an idiot.

If you are wondering whether to tell or not tell, call a crisis center or helpline and get advice. If your friend told you he was thinking of suicide, you must assume that the part of him that wants to live was asking for help. You can't ignore that.

David told me that he felt he had more options as he grew older. That, of course, is true. Teens have more ability to get out into the community, more contacts with helping agencies, more freedom to come and go, a job and perhaps more money to do things than they did when they were younger, but they don't have less need for suicide unless they have dealt with their problems, or their problems have diminished. Sometimes just living longer and living through problems makes teens understand that they have a lot of inner strength. But sometimes time doesn't give them those answers. They still have the same problems with parents whether they are sixteen or thirty-six. They still feel a low self-esteem. They still feel unimportant, and unwanted.

I know that many of you felt alone, ignored and invisible in society, but I was impressed by the many people who did care about you. The teens that answered my ad in the newspaper wanted to help you. The crisis center personnel in Vancouver, Toronto, and Halifax really wanted to do something to help. The business people who ran the foundations that gave me the money to go across Canada and talk to you really cared about what happened to you. The Canadian Mental Health Association, a group that is made up of people who care, helped a great deal. In fact there were so many people who cared about teens and who wanted to make this book a hand reaching out, that I felt as if there was a strong network waiting for all teens in trouble if they could only reach for it. We all want teens to believe that there is someone near who cares. There is someone who will help. Keep trying until you find that someone.

EPILOG

What I Learned — Parents are important.

I hadn't realized how important parents are. They seem to have tremendous power to make you feel inferior. I didn't realize that when you are thirteen through to adulthood the feelings parents show you, the reflection parents give you of yourself, influences you profoundly. I thought that teenage suicide was social problem. You told me it was a family problem. Some of you chose suicide because it seemed a socially acceptable way to get rid of pain. You *may* have had problems with your social group but your pull to suicide seemed to be directly related to rejection by your family, not to rejection by your social group.

I learned that I was as capable of ignoring teens' feelings as some of your parents. I empathized with you. I could see how your parents had made life difficult for you and yet I realized that I had said some of the things to my children that your parents had said to you. At different times in my children's lives I had some of the same attitudes that your parents did. I had slipped into some of the same patterns. You made me re-think my relationships with my own children.

I expected to find that your suicidal feelings stemmed from the pressures of competition, maybe a shallow social environment, a lack of direction and goals—almost anything. I had an open mind on suicide. I had no idea what you thought was hard in your lives. You told me. What was hard to live with was the attitude of your parents. Generally, if your parents accepted you, you could deal with life. If they didn't, you couldn't.

I learned from you that low self-esteem, feeling worthless, valueless, is not a permanent personality trait. Many of you moved out of the difficult downward spiral of diminishing self-esteem to find confidence and appreciation of your personality. Self-esteem isn't a black and white situation, a positive or negative only. It is a continuum. Self-esteem moves from very low to very high even in the same person, sometimes in a short period. If you have low self-esteem now, that doesn't mean you will always have low self-esteem. You told me you learned, slowly, over time, to like yourself.

Very often, suicide attempts happened after a loss that took a long time to deal with. Psychologists suggest that it takes at least six weeks for most people to begin to feel better after a loss —*begin* to feel better. It might be months or a year before the pain fades. Many of you had no idea that you were expected to feel badly about a loss for so long a time and were overwhelmed by your feelings.

You felt a pressure to be happy, to be an expression of your family's worth by seeming to be happy. You often saw happiness evaluated by your parents in terms of things: money, houses, jobs, status. You saw that your parents expected you to achieve academically and in the work force with a "good" job or a "good" career. But you saw little room in the job market for you, little chance of success in your parents' plan for you. Still, it wasn't your perception of the job market that was overwhelming, it was your parents' expectations of "super success." You saw little time to find your own way. Parents and teachers told you that you had to hurry. You had to compete. You had to be in the top twenty percent or you wouldn't get a job, you'd be a nobody. You knew you couldn't do it.

So very often, no one asked you what *you* wanted, or how soon you wanted it. No one asked how you were coping, or helped you deal with pressures. I asked Diana and Steven if anyone in their entire life had ever sat down beside them and asked, "What's wrong?" They looked at each other, reflected on their lives then said that they didn't think so. They were usually *told* what was wrong with them. They had no chance to work out their problems with an understanding adult.

Your life at school seemed too hard. You friends superficial. At home, you were accepted only when you met your parents' expectations. You were accepted for the things you did well, your achievements. You were not accepted just because you existed. Your parents often demanded that you earn their love. That seemed forever unattainable to you. What you needed was parents who loved you and accepted you because they valued you, not because you earned that love in a daily merit system. If unearned love was not available to you, you believed you were not "good enough." You were not the person they wanted. You would never be the person they wanted. Such a dangerous family situation made suicide attractive.

To break such a pattern in your life you needed to understand that the pattern existed. You needed to face it and you needed to talk about it; you needed someone to talk to.

You taught me that most of the time help, a life-line, a way out, doesn't just happen. Someone outside yourself, a friend, a crisis center worker, a psychologist, someone, made an effort. Someone listened while you talked, while you poured out your frustrations, worries, nightmares. In talking you faced your problems and slowly worked your way through to a solution. You weren't asking for great teen centers. You weren't asking for a counselor for every classroom. You weren't asking for a course in suicide. You weren't asking for a huge social service rescue committee. You needed one friend. You needed society to produce one friend for each of you. You needed to look into the world around you and pull out one friend. That's what you wanted, someone to talk to. You would prefer to talk to someone who was near your own age, who had been through the trauma of attempted suicide, who could understand and support you. These qualifications of an effective counselor describe what you can be to someone else. *You* can counsel another teen. The responsibility for caring about teens lies with you, the teens. You do need to care enough about each other to help. You are the most powerful force for change. By being a friend, by being there to talk to, teenagers themselves can prevent suicide in others.

One of the encouraging things about the human race is its capacity for change. Personalities, ideas and abilities to cope can change from day to day or week to week. The world can change too. What one faces today can change, dramatically or slowly, from a suffocating, destructive environment to an encouraging, support-ive one. A person can change from self-destructive and withdrawn to loving and comfortable. The possibility is there. People, by virtue of being human, are capable of that.

So many of you could not deal with your parents. Often you felt distant from your fathers. You wanted a warm relationship with both parents but you couldn't see how to make that happen. You may never have the kind of relationship you want with your parents, but you may have a better one than you do right now. Don't give up on them. They also are capable of change. They may learn to listen.

Most of you had changed. Life did get better for you. If others, the ones who are gone, had not completed their suicides, life might have changed for them. They needed more time, more friends, more hope.

You showed me time after time your caring, your sensitivity, your social responsibility. You impressed me over and over with your strength, your determination and your tremendous courage. I wish I could hold you in reserve and send you to every teen who contemplates suicide because you would show them how much you care, you would understand, and help. Perhaps it will help those who are reading this to know that you are there, thirty of you, hoping for them, caring, wishing them courage and the strength to help themselves.

QUESTIONNAIRE

1. **Stats:**

   Name: Age: Sex:

   Family: Position in the family:

2. **Living Arrangements:**

   at home
        with 2 parents?   1 parent?   sibling(s)?

        away from home
        with a friend?   partner?   alone?

3. **Rate the strength of your relationships**(10 is good, 1 is bad)

   Now:
        with your mother?   with your father?

        with each member of your family?

        with a special friend?

Just before suicide:

with your mother?   with your father?

with each member of your family?

with your special friend?

How does your family handle emotions:

anger?   guilt?   love?

How do you handle emotions:

4. **Tell me about your suicide attempt.**

5. **Precipitating Factors—Trigger Events**

What happened on the day of the suicide attempt?

Was that usual?   unusual?

What happened that made suicide seem like a way to solve your problems (family, school, social problems or problems of society like nuclear war):

that day?

before that day?

Why did suicide seem like an option?

Why was it the only thing that you thought would work?

What else could you have done?

Do you still think suicide is an option to the problems of living, that it is one way to solve problems?

6. **What did you expect to happen after your suicide:**

What did happen?

What do you wish had happened?

Did you see a doctor?   Did he/she help?

7. **What was you life like before you tried suicide?**
daily routine

sports

social

family

8. **Success**
Did you see yourself as,

successful at most things:

or

a failure at most things:

How do you see yourself now?

9. **How many times have you tried suicide?**
Events before your first suicide attempt:

Age: Family at the time:

Did anyone know you were going to try suicide?

Who?

How did they know?

Does this person carry guilt about this?

10. **Did your attempt at suicide shock your parents?**

How did they react?

11. **Had anyone in your family tried suicide?:**

Before you did?   After you did?

Does your family talk about it?

Has anyone in your family died in a suicide?

Has any friend of yours died in a suicide?

12. **What was your usual day like just before you tried suicide:**

What kinds of things made you feel better?

Why couldn't you do those "feel better" things at the time?

What kinds of thing made you feel worse?

13. **What changes occurred in your life after the suicide attempt?**

14. **What do you think others (parents, siblings, friends) should have done for you or with you?**

15. What do you wish would change in your life?

Do you feel:

you can make changes?

that you have the power to change things?

16. What needed to change in your life before suicide was no longer an option?

What do you think needs to change in the world before suicide stops being an option for teens?

If you were thinking of committing suicide right now what would change your mind?:

What could your parents do?

What could you do?

What could other family members do?

What could your friends do?

What could anyone else do?

17. If you were thinking of committing suicide right now, who would you talk to:

a friend?   a sister or brother?

a parent?   the school counselor?

the crisis center?   a doctor?

someone else?

18. Do your friends talk about suicide?

If not, why not?

Has any friend talked to you about committing suicide?

How does talking about suicide make them feel?

Did you talk to anyone when you thought of trying suicide?

If not, why not?

If you had a "Youth Line" in your town, would you have used it?

19. Right now, do you feel:

that you belong in your family?

necessary to your family?

important to your friends?

20. Just before you tried suicide, did you feel:

that you belonged in your family?

that you were necessary to your family?

that your friends needed you?

21. When you thought about trying suicide, how long did you think about it:

a few minutes?

a day?

a week?

a month?

a year?

years?

22. When you thought about trying suicide where did you think about it:

at home?

at school?

when you were alone?

BIBLIOGRAPHY

Books

Alvarez, A., *The Savage God, A Study of Suicide,* Random House, New York, 1972

Baechler, Jean, *Suicides,* Basic Books, Inc., New York, 1975

Callwood, June, *Emotions,* Doubleday of Canada, Toronto, 1986

Evoy, John Joseph, *The Rejected, Psychological Consequences of Parental Rejection,* The Pennsylvania State University Press, University Park and London, 1981

Giovachini, Peter, *The Urge to Die, Why Young People Commit Suicide,* MacMillan Co., New York, 1981

Gordon, Sol, *When Living Hurts,* Union of American Hebrew Congregations, New York, 1985

Hendin, Herbert, *Suicide in America,* W. W. Norton & Co., New York, 1982

Hyde, Margaret and Elizabeth Held Forsyth, *The Hidden Epidemic,* Franklin Watts, New York, London, 1978

Klagsbrun, Francine, *Too Young to Die,* Houghton Mifflin Co., Boston, 1976

Lester, David, *Why People Kill Themselves, Summary of Research Findings on Suicidal Behavior,* 2nd ed., Charles C. Thomas, Springfield, IL, 1983

Mack, John E., and H. Hickler, *Vivienne, The Life and Suicide of an Adolescent Girl,* Little, Boston, 1981

Maris, Ronald W., *Pathways to Suicide,* John Hopkins University Press, Baltimore, MD, 1981

Pfeffer, Cynthia R., *The Suicidal Child,* The Guilford Press, New York, London, 1986

Reynolds, David K., and Norman L. Farberow, *The Family Shadow, Sources of Suicide and Schizophrenia,* University of California Press, Berkeley, Los Angeles, London, 1981

Richman, Joseph, *Family Therapy for Suicidal People,* Springer Publishing Company, New York, 1986

Rosenfeld, Linda, and Marilynne Prupas, *Left Alive, After a Suicide Death in the Family,* Charles C. Thomas, Springfield, IL, 1984

Sanderson, J.D., *How to Stop Worrying About Your Kids,* W. W. Norton & Co, New York, 1978

Scarfe, Maggie, *Intimate Partners, Patterns in Love and Marriage,* Random House, New York, 1987

Stengel, Erwin, *Suicide and Attempted Suicide,* Jason Aronson, New York, 1974

Tavris, Carol, *Anger, The Misunderstood Emotion,* A Touchstone Book, Simon and Schuster, New York, 1982

Viorst, Judith, *Necessary Losses, The Loves, Illusions, Dependencies and Impossible*

Expectations that All of Us Have to Give Up in Order to Grow, Fawcett Gold Medal, New York, 1986

Periodicals

Bagley, Christopher, and Richard Ramsay, "Problems and Priorities in Research on Suicidal Behavior: An Overview with Canadian Implications," *Canadian Journal of Community Mental Health,* Vol. 4, No. 1, Spring 1985

"Listen to Me, A Guide for Youth on Depression and Suicide," *Canadian Mental Health Association*

"The Impact of Suicide in Television Movies," *The New England Journal of Medicine,* Sept. 11, 1986, p. 690

Konopka, Gisela, "Adolescent Suicide," *Exceptional Children,* Vol. 49 (5) Feb. 1983, p. 390-94

Pettifor, J., Perry, D., Plowman, B., and S. Pitcher, "Risk Factors Prediction Childhood and Adolescent Suicides," *Journal of Child Care,* Vol. 1 (3) Jan. 1983, p. 17-49

Pfeffer, Dr. Cynthia, *Minneapolis Star and Tribune,* United Press, May 15, 1987

Public Affairs Report, University of California, Berkeley, Vol 25, No. 1, Feb. 1984

"Suicide in Canada, Report of the National Task Force on Suicide in Canada," Sponsored by the Mental Health Division, Health Services and Promotion Branch, Health and Welfare Canada, Published by Minister of National Health and Welfare, 1987

Westwood, Michael, "The Health of Canadian Youth, a Developmental Perspective," *Health Promotion,* Winter 1986

Zimmerman, Joy, "Teenage Suicide," *Pacific Sun,* Morin, California, April 10-16, 1987, p. 356 and 12

Also available from NC Press

THE FACE IN THE MIRROR
Teenagers Talk About Adoption

Marion Crook
ISBN 0-920053-67-x, 128 pages, paper, $9.95
Video Tape Available $29.95 including tax where applicable

"I just want to know why I was given up. That's all," Karen pressed her hands on the table and leaned towards me, "I just want to know why."

Written especially for the adopted teenager, as well as parents and caregivers, *The Face in the Mirror* examines the ways young people, adopted in the last twenty years, are dealing with the complex relationships in their lives and the adoption issues facing society today.

Teenagers want to know • why were they "given away" • what kind of family their birth mother came from • what their birth mother is like • their medical history

"I was prepared to find you polite and a little distant. I was, after all, somebody's mother. So I was pleased and grateful that you were so frank and so willing to talk... Sometimes you told me quietly, sometimes emphatically; but you wanted to tell me and, through me, other teenagers what it is like to be adopted. I became a vehicle of your expression and this book is yours." The Author

The Face in the Mirror Video Tape, based on the interviews in the book, provides a moving introduction to any discussion of adoptions issues today.

ORDER FORM

Please send me:

___ copies of **Face in the Mirror**   @ $9.95 $ _____

___ copies of **Face in the Mirror Video Tape**   @ $29.95 $ _____

Format _____   Shipping and handling $ 2.00

        Enclosed please find my cheque payable to NC Press Limited for $ _____

Please bill my   ☐ VISA   ☐ Mastercard _____

Signature _____

      Expiry Date _____ / _____

Name _____

Address _____

City _____ Prov/State _____ Postal Code _____

Mail to,
In Canada: NC Press, 401, 260 Richmond Street W, Toronto, ON, M5V 1W5
In U.S.A.: NC Press, 170 Broadway, Ste. 201, New York City, NY, 10038